Academic Quality Assurance In Irish Higher Education:

ELEMENTS OF A HANDBOOK

Thomas Duff
Academic Registrar
Dublin Institute of Technology (DIT)

Joseph Hegarty
Head, School of Culinary Arts and Food Technology
DIT Cathal Brugha Street

Matthew Hussey
Director, Faculty of Science
DIT Kevin Street

BLACKHALL
Publishing

This book was typeset by
Gough Typesetting Services for
Blackhall Publishing
8 Priory Hall,
Stillorgan, Co. Dublin,
Ireland

e-mail: blackhall@eircom.net
www.blackhallpublishing.com

ISBN: 1 842180 14 2

A catalogue record for this book is
available from the British Library.

Printed in Ireland by
ColourBooks Ltd

Dedication

This book is dedicated:

to colleagues and former colleagues in the Dublin Institute of Technology who have striven and continue to strive to provide education of the highest quality to the Institute's students;

and especially to Michael O'Donnell, formerly deputy President, acting President and Director of the Institute, who pioneered the systematic development of quality assurance procedures across the schools and other units of the Dublin Institute of Technology.

Contents

Preface

Quality assurance has been a feature of higher education in a wide range of countries for some twenty years. It has also been in operation to an extent in the regional Institutes of Technology (formerly Regional Technical Colleges) and the Dublin Institute of Technology for all of that time, albeit not under the heading of "quality assurance". Recent legislation proposes that such procedures be implemented throughout the higher education system in Ireland in the coming years.

This book outlines the history and development of academic quality assurance internationally, introduces the issues that have emerged and recommends appropriate guideline procedures. It is directed primarily at the staff of the higher education institutions, universities, institutes of technology and others, to clarify and demystify the issues involved. The book should also be of interest to local and national government and agency officials who oversee the institutions and seek to improve their effectiveness. It is also hoped that the book will be of use to students of the higher educational system at home and abroad.

May 2000

Introduction

Higher education in the Republic of Ireland has experienced unprecedented growth and change over the past thirty years. This has resulted in changes in the nature of the higher education institutions and in their relationship with society. Increasingly over the past decade, the Irish government has focused attention on quality issues. It is safe to predict that increasingly over the coming decade, quality assurance will become an integral part of the ethos and practice of all the higher education institutions.

As early as 1994 the director of higher level education in the Department of Education summarised the motivations behind the government's interest in quality assurance.[1] These were:

- the quality assurance developments in the industrial and business sector and the emergence of ISO 9000 and total quality management (TQM)

- concern about the growth in public sector expenditure

- a developing pressure to rank programmes and institutions according to some priority criteria

- the huge expansion of the higher education system

- the greater openness and awareness in society

- concern for transparency and accountability in the application of public expenditures

- the Controller and Auditor General Act 1993, which sought to achieve greater efficiency, effectiveness and value for money in public expenditures

- the increased international mobility of students, researchers and teachers and the need for international recognition of standards and qualifications

- the developing internationalisation of the European labour market.

In recent legislation — the Universities Act 1997 and the Qualifications

---

[1] McDonagh, P, *Emerging Issues in Quality Assurance in Irish Higher Education*, Seminar on Self-Regulatory Approach to Quality Assurance, Dublin Institute of Technology (Dublin), May 1994.

(Education and Training) Act 1999 in particular — the government has called for quality assurance processes to become integral to the work of the higher education institutions in the future. With this legislative framework in place, the coming decade will see these processes acquiring increased importance and influence in the delivery of higher education in Ireland.

ACADEMIC QUALITY

Academic quality can not be specifically defined, but may be broadly outlined in comparative terms. It encompasses concepts of standards, excellence, effectiveness, value for money and so-called fitness for purpose. The International Organisation for Standardisation has offered a formal definition of quality as "the totality of characteristics of an entity that bear on its ability to satisfy stated and implied needs".[2]

Setting and maintaining standards in higher education involve accepting the existence of calibrated standards or benchmarks against which the standards achieved in a given institution can be compared. The benchmarks must be widely acknowledged, especially by the students and other stakeholders. Furthermore, the standards must be objectively quantifiable and measurable, or at least reasonably objectively comparable with the benchmarks, by reliable and experienced observers.

Clearly the standards set must refer to the level, appropriateness and effectiveness of each element of an academic programme to the aims and objectives of that programme. Excellence must be viewed in the same light. The assessment and comparison of different parameters of the educational process require clear understanding of the purposes of education, considerable experience of a variety of different higher education institutions and thorough training and preparation. These aspects are vital for an acceptable quality system.

The concept of quality relies on involvement by stakeholders — clients, consumers and customers — in helping to determine standards. There are many stakeholders in higher education, each often seeking different outcomes, some of which may be in conflict. The main stakeholders are students, but the following are also significant:

- parents of students

- alumnae/alumni

- staff members — academic, administrative and other — of the institution itself

---

[2] International Organisation for Standardisation: ISO 8402, *Quality Management and Quality Assurance — Vocabulary* (Geneva) 1994.

- the broader academic and professional community
- the local and national governments and the European Union
- other funding bodies
- business and industrial organisations
- the local and national communities.

Furthermore, the concept of quality applies to all the activities and human and physical resources that combine to underpin the academic programmes of the institution. Excellent teaching and learning require excellent teachers, excellent students, excellent facilities, excellent programmes and excellent management and support in an ethos of academic excellence.

Quality assurance is a process through which a higher education institution guarantees to itself and its stakeholders that its teaching, learning and other services consistently reach a standard of excellence. Such assurance is a necessary goal for the institution itself. Increasingly, it is also necessary for publicly funded institutions to be accountable, and provide assurances, to society and the state that they are delivering the services for which they are funded, thus ensuring that they are providing value for money.

Therefore quality assurance incorporates all the processes internal to the institution, whereby quality is evaluated, maintained and improved.

The process by which each part or stage of a service, such as education, is compared and checked against an agreed standard benchmark and either accepted or rejected, is called quality control. Therefore, quality control normally requires procedures and 'calibrated' standards, including procedures for correction when standards are not achieved, at a number of stages along the sequence of stages involved in delivering the service.

The overall process by which an institution is managed to achieve and assure quality in its services is called quality management or total quality management (TQM). This involves quality control at a number of key stages, specifying and documenting standards and procedures, identifying responsibilities and lines of responsibility, reporting, training and retraining of all staff and regular checking and remedying of failures or shortfalls. The key feature of TQM is the agreement with stakeholders on the intermediate and final standards. When applied to higher education, this approach concerns all activities and all sections and staff of the institution — academic, technical, administrative and other support staff.

A quality audit is a review, generally by an authorised organisation external to the higher education institution itself, of the procedures and mechanisms of quality assurance and management within the institution. It allows the outside organisation to assure stakeholders, including students and their parents as well as the government and society in general, that claimed standards and quality are consistently achieved within the institution.

A step beyond quality audit is quality assessment, where an authorised organisation external to the institution evaluates the quality and standards aimed for and achieved by the institution and declares that these quality and standards do or do not reach the levels generally achieved in comparable institutions elsewhere in higher education.

Benchmarking is an activity or process requiring that the best practice in the activity be identified. A best practice, or a world class practice, in a higher education activity is one which is widely acknowledged as one that gives optimum performance. This performance is generally across a range of criteria and performance indices, such as value for money, simplicity, best service, reliability of data and a high percentage of successful students and graduates. A chosen best practice is studied and adapted and applied to the corresponding activity in the institution. The resulting performance criteria are then measured in the institution and compared to the acknowledged best practice. Areas where the performance falls below best practice are then steadily improved, resulting in enhancement on the overall activity.

Peer review is a key aspect of academic quality assurance and quality audit. Within an institution internal peer review comes into play in departmental meetings, in the work of course committees and teams designing and planning a course, conducting the course, jointly assessing the work of students and deciding on student performance in examination boards, in joint research projects and the work of research groups, and in the meetings of faculty and institutional committees and working groups. In all of these situations, colleagues from different disciplines and with different academic and industrial backgrounds share and compare experiences and evaluations. The development and optimisation of internal peer review can be served best by the continual facilitation and encouragement of partnership, co-operation and teamwork at department, faculty and institution level.

Such internal peer review contains an element of benchmarking, containing as it does comparison between experiences of external institutions and their practices and those of the institution itself.

External peer review occurs particularly when external academic and industrial, business or professional experts participate formally in course validation and review panels and as external examiners for programmes. Such external peers bring with them the experience of their own organisations and of other institutions with which they have been associated and again provide a vital element of benchmarking in their work. Visits of external experts to an institution, as visiting lecturers or as consultants on research projects, course development or other academic matters, also provide valuable elements of benchmarking.

Sabbatical leave, temporary placement in industry or business and visits by staff members to other academic institutions and to academic events such as conferences and workshops, also provide opportunities for comparisons and for obtaining insights on other approaches aimed at improving standards and performance within the institution. Many such insights can also be found in library research and in the study of institutional web sites on the internet.

In each such case, however, in order for some element of benchmarking to be achieved it is essential that the experiences and the comparisons be articulated as objectively as possible, formally presented to colleagues and thoroughly discussed and disseminated.

Monitoring and maintaining quality are clearly the fundamental personal quest of each individual teacher and each other member of staff in an institution. If this is not the case, it is difficult if not impossible to achieve quality in the team enterprise of course delivery. It is a key task of academic management to establish the team and to develop the individual staff members as a cohesive group, with unity and clarity of purpose, and identified with the institution's mission and strategic plan. For this reason higher education institutions have developed mission statements and elaborated strategic plans to help set in place that partnership, unity of purpose and sharing of values required to deliver the best service to students and society. In this context, higher education institutions have come to realise that while selecting the most qualified staff possible is necessary, this is not, in itself, sufficient, and carefully planned and continuous staff development and training are also a key requirement in ensuring the delivery of quality.

These and related issues form the themes of this book.

OUTLINE OF THE BOOK

An outline of the changes in higher education internationally, the factors giving rise to them and how they bring quality assurance issues to the fore, is provided in Chapter 1.

In Chapter 2 the complex processes of teaching, research and learning in higher education, which academic quality assurance procedures seek to evaluate and improve, are reviewed.

In order to develop the international context of the movement towards quality assurance in higher education institutions, Chapter 3 describes the development of quality assurance concepts and procedures in higher education across Europe and elsewhere. The role of bodies such as the European Union and other international organisations in this process is considerable.

Chapter 4 outlines the increasingly confident steps taken by Irish governments in recent years, through policy statements, regulation and legislation, to introduce quality assurance and quality audit processes in all Irish higher education institutions

An outline of typical quality assurance and improvement procedures and guidelines for an individual course is given in Chapter 5 which considers initial validation, and in Chapter 6 which considers course operation.

Chapters 7 and 8 suggest appropriate procedures and practices for quality assurance in postgraduate research work.

The physical, administrative and management framework for quality within a higher education institution is treated in Chapter 9.

The requirements and procedures for a departmental, faculty or institutional quality audit are considered in Chapter 10.

Chapter 11 reviews some of the key issues that have emerged in the international debate about quality assurance and quality audit in higher education and develops the case for actively and constructively implementing these procedures in the Irish institutions.

CHAPTER ONE

The Changing Nature of Higher Education

Higher education in the Republic of Ireland has experienced unprecedented growth and change over the past thirty years. In Britain, a similar process was experienced soon after World War II and accelerated in the 1960s. The analogous process had begun earlier this century in the United States and accelerated there also in the post World War II period. The expansion and diversification in Ireland has been particularly complex in that, over the same period, there have been rapid and significant developments in technology and communications, as well as in Irish society itself.

This chapter outlines the development of higher education in Ireland and sets it in the general context of economic and technological change. It examines the resulting changes in the nature of the higher education institutions and their relationship with society, factors which fuel the need for quality assurance procedures in the institutions.

THE EMERGENCE OF QUALITY ASSURANCE IN HIGHER EDUCATION

Resulting from the social, physical and intellectual changes during the past generation, many aspects of higher education have come increasingly under public scrutiny. In Britain, Western Europe, Australia and the United States, this scrutiny has been conducted under a broad social, technological, economic and political framework expressed mainly in the demand for academic quality assurance procedures internal to the higher educational institutions, and for accreditation or quality audit of the institutions by external authorities. In these countries, academic quality assurance has, over the past fifteen to twenty years, become the paradigm by which higher education institutions seek to present and justify the effectiveness and relevance of their programmes and activities. Academic quality assurance has also tended to provide the criteria whereby the outside world — principally the government, but also industry, business and society in general — can evaluate the role and contribution of these institutions.

As quality assurance has assumed greater significance within higher education internationally it has helped to stimulate thinking on a range of other issues which relate to the essential nature of higher education, its processes and institutions. Such issues include:

- the purpose of education

- the ways in which the higher education institution serves society and who decides this

- the complex processes of teaching and learning and their evaluation

- the development of appropriate knowledge, skills and competencies among staff to enable them to enhance their performance as teachers

- the key characteristics, in terms of knowledge, skills and competencies, of a graduate of a course of study

- the role, functions and accountability of the higher education institution in society

- academic freedom and autonomy within the institution

- the effectiveness and transparency of institutional governance

- the general relationships between the institution and society

- the duty of the institution to promote social inclusion

- the responsibility of the institution in relation to social, ethical and other goals of society

- the relationship between the institution and the professions and business/ industry.

In the Republic of Ireland, despite many changes and developments, academic quality assurance and quality audit procedures have not yet been applied systematically to higher education. However, the emphasis placed on quality assurance in the Universities Act 1997 and the Qualifications (Education and Training) Act 1999 with its plan for a new national qualifications authority, indicates that these procedures, and the consequent fundamental rethinking of higher education activities will, in the future, be a significant aspect of the work of the higher education institutions in Ireland.[1]

---

[1] *Charting our Education Future*, White Paper (Baile Átha Cliath: Oifig an tSoláthair) 1995, p. 108.

DEVELOPMENT OF MASS HIGHER EDUCATION IN IRELAND

Higher education in Ireland since the late 1960s and early 1970s has been characterised by the establishment and development of new institutions, further development of the existing ones, increasing funding provided by government and increasing mass participation.

The 1995 White Paper on education referred to the significant increase in government spending on higher education since the 1960s, as shown in Table 1.1.[2] Even with the accompanying increase in the numbers of students in higher education, there is growing pressure to achieve greater value for money.

Table 1.1 Approximate annual government current and capital expenditure and current and total expenditure per undergraduate student (normalised to 1995 values) on higher education at mid-decade since the 1960s

Year	Current expenditure	Capital expenditure	Current expenditure per student	Total expenditure per student
1965	£ 5m	£11m	£ 300	£ 800
1975	£ 40m	£27m	£1,300	£2,200
1985	£190m	£25m	£3,800	£4,300
1995	£430m	£36m	£4,700	£5,100

Also there has been a growing emphasis on research and development work within the higher education institutions over the past twenty years or so and an increase in annual funding for this activity from £16m to £48m between 1982 and 1992.

Full time student enrolments in higher education in the Republic of Ireland have been growing steadily since the end of World War II. Table 1.2 shows the historical percentage of each yearly cohort entering full time higher education at mid-decade since 1965. As reported by Clancy, these enrolments have been rising by 26 per cent to 38 per cent every half decade since 1960.[3] The total number enrolled in 1965 was 18,500 and by 1995 that number had risen to 92,000. The Steering Committee on the Future Development of Higher Education has projected that these enrolments, if not capped, will increase

[2] *Ibid.,* p. 90.
[3] Clancy, P, *Who goes to College? A Second National Survey of Participation in Higher Education* (Dublin: Higher Education Authority) 1988.

further to the year 2015, as shown in Table 1.2.[4] The report of the Steering Committee projected these increases by taking into account demographic trends and the plans of the government to continue to increase the percentage of each yearly cohort of leaving certificate students embarking on full-time higher education.

Table 1.2 Total numbers enrolled in full time higher education and the percentage of each yearly cohort entering full time higher education, in each mid-decade year from 1965 to 1995 and projected to 2015

Year	Total number of enrolments	Percentage of age cohort enrolling
1965	19,000	11%
1975	30,000	19%
1985	50,000	28%
1995	92,000	45%
2005	120,000	51%
2015	118,000	53%

The report of the Steering Committee also recommended that the 1995 level of capital funding for higher education, £36m, be increased to £45m annually from 1996 to 2000 and be maintained at £36m annually from 2001 to 2005. It also recommended the doubling of the annual allocation for equipment in the higher education institutions from about £5m in 1995 to £10m in 1999.

Early in 1996, a study on the present and projected supply of and demand for personnel in the information technology (IT) sector, suggested that by 2000 there would be a deficit of 125 per cent in degree graduates and 25 per cent in certificate and diploma graduates in this area in the country.[5] The study recommended that the government should support the necessary expansion in the institutions, in addition to the allocations above, to prevent these deficits.

The overriding characteristic of higher education in Ireland is therefore one of expansion and diversification. This is projected to continue into the

---

[4] *Report of the Steering Committee on the Future Development of Higher Education (Based on a Study of Needs to the Year 2015)* (Dublin: Higher Education Authority) 1995.
[5] Stokes, P A and M McGarry, *Supply and Demand for IT Personnel in Ireland 1996-2000* (Dublin) 1996.

next decade to cater for both demographic changes and government priorities. The rapidly increasing participation rates in higher education signal a fundamental change from the previous elite emphasis to a more universal or mass system. The change is much more than a quantitative one. In recruiting into higher education large numbers of students with a wider range of academic skills and abilities and from a wider socio-economic range than ever before, it has made a fundamental societal change and a revolutionary change in the institutions themselves.

It is essential that these changes and developments occur, but not at the expense of academic standards and quality. In 1995, the Steering Committee on the Future Development of Higher Education recognised the need for resource allocation adequate for an effective system of quality assurance for public accountability and transparency and for "continuing confirmation and validation of academic standards". It offered the following recommendations in relation to the quality assurance system required:

- it should be flexible

- it should minimise any bureaucratic requirements of reporting

- it should ensure accountability and transparency

- it should encourage trust, based on integrity and professionalism

- the "core element" of such system should be "that of self-evaluation supported by peer review and quality audit"

- support should be provided "for staff development as a key element in the evaluation of quality"

- "concerned interests, including staff and students, should be consulted in the development" of the system to ensure these developments.

Also in 1995, the White Paper on education highlighted how quality assurance in higher education would benefit students, society and the economy, in that it would underpin the "status and mobility of graduates both nationally and internationally". It outlined how quality assurance would bring the possible contradiction between accountability and autonomy to the fore, because while there must be accountability for the efficient use of public funds, the control of core academic freedom and associated matters should still rest with the higher education institutions themselves. It also indicated that quality assurance procedures in higher education in Ireland would, in the future, be developed with due recognition of:

- the institutions' primary responsibility to create a quality culture and develop and implement their own quality assurance procedures

- these procedures being adequate and involving "rigorous peer review"

- the need for accountability and transparency to the public in respect of quality and value for money

- the respective rights and responsibilities of the government and the individual institutions.

The White Paper projected that the Higher Education Authority (HEA) would continue to develop quality auditing systems that would feature:

- monitoring the quality assurance systems within the individual institutions

- periodic internal self-evaluation of teaching, research and links with the wider community of faculties and departments in the institutions followed by their evaluation by panels composed of national and international peers

- development of suitable quantitative and/or qualitative indicators of performance to allow national and international comparison

- monitoring of the findings of these evaluations and the implementation of any recommendations of the evaluation process

- publication of the findings of the evaluations and the use of the findings in developing policy at HEA and Department of Education levels.

As a key complement to the quality assurance and quality audit procedures envisaged, the White Paper also set as a priority the development of a comprehensive programme for improving teaching skills in higher education.

CHANGES IN INFORMATION TECHNOLOGY AND THE ECONOMY

The information technology revolution — the emergence of digital computers, their dissemination to the personal level, their application to the multiplicity of tasks in every area of life and their interconnection through global communication networks — has been underway for over thirty years. Over this period there has been the parallel and profoundly inter-linked revolution in electronic telecommunications — radio, television and video, telephony and multimedia. Virtually every form of medium can now be made available in electronic form on a global scale. The nature of information storage, retrieval and availability has been completely changed in a single generation.

This change has profound implications for higher education institutions. Since information is now so readily available in electronic form, the processes of teaching and learning can not remain as they were. The processes of knowledge transfer also are changing continuously. The nature and extent of the knowledge acquisition required of students in different disciplines are also changing continuously. The ways in which information can now be obtained and used are much more varied than was the case even thirty years ago. The evolution of the library towards a remotely accessed electronic resource serves to emphasise these points.

Furthermore, higher education institutions provide education for the future leaders in the exploitation of the products of the information and communications revolution. For this reason, these institutions must be intimately involved and proactive in applying the most advanced technology solutions possible to the issues of teaching, research, learning and general administration.

Since the 1960s, the Irish economy has been progressively opened to world trade. Incentives such as low corporation taxation and the availability of an educated workforce have been used to attract industrial and trading companies to establish in Ireland.

The provision of an appropriately educated workforce has shaped government policy in education, including higher education, and continues to do so. Global competition therefore comes to bear on education as well as on the industrial and business sectors.

Ireland's membership of the European Union (EU) has helped to mediate this influence on education in that the EU seeks to develop co-operation between institutions and student and graduate mobility between the member states. Academic excellence, comparability of standards and mutual recognition of awards are fundamental in this regard.

International competition inexorably drives industries and educational institutions to strive to be more effective and efficient than their competitors. In the higher education sector, this increasingly requires an ethos of continuous improvement or "kaizen" — a Japanese word denoting "perpetual improvement". This reality, probably more than any other, impels the higher education system towards quality assurance and quality audit. Even in the limited context of the island of Ireland, where the higher education institutions of Northern Ireland are subjected to the rigorous quality assurance and quality auditing processes of the British Quality Assurance Agency, it is an imperative for those in the Republic of Ireland to implement similar quality processes in order to remain competitive.

NATURE OF THE CLASSICAL OR TRADITIONAL UNIVERSITY

Contrary to the image of the "ivory tower", the classical university had a strong professional character from its beginnings in the late Middle Ages in Bologna, Paris and Oxford. It prepared its graduates for the pursuit of knowledge and learning and for a range of occupations including the clerical, legal, educational and medical professions. With its evolution and redefinition by such figures as von Humboldt and Newman during the 19th century, the university developed new dimensions and values other than those related directly to employment of graduates.[6] While not abandoning its professional disciplines, it tended to be characterised by the pursuit of knowledge and learning for their own sake, often with little regard for the practical application of that knowledge.[7]

Fields or disciplines of knowledge, rather than problems in society or industry, came to define teaching and research in these institutions. Academics assumed the right to define the contents of study programmes and indeed the mission and purpose of their institutions. Teacher knew best. The freedom of the academics to pursue their interests and specialised subjects and to disseminate their discoveries and insights came to signify the fundamental autonomy or academic freedom of their institution. In such institutions innovation and change were not high priorities. The institutions were characterised by an independence and an aloofness or "ivory-tower" attitude, somewhat remote from contemporary society and events.

Perhaps no university perfectly matched this model and in the 19th century some, such as the University of London (which helped to inspire the structure of the Queen's Colleges in Ireland in the late 1840s) and the land-grant colleges in the United States after the American Civil War, departed quite radically from it.[8] Government pressures for reform and the establishment on the European mainland of technical universities during the 19th and early 20th centuries paved the way for further change.

In the course of the 20th century and most markedly over the past thirty years, the university has been changed dramatically from an institution offering education to an elite to one offering education to the masses. This has led to a new description of "modern university" or even "'post-modern university" being posited.[9] Higher education in most of the countries of the world has been caught up in these processes of change.

The expansion and diversification of universities and other higher education institutions around the world has caused a fundamental questioning of the nature, function and role of these institutions in society. The accelerating changes in information technology, the nature of knowledge, communications and knowledge acquisition, have all added to this questioning. This debate has flowered particularly in Britain, where the changes have been

---

[6] McGrath, F, *Newman's University: Ideas and Reality* (Dublin) 1951.

[7] Skilbeck, M and H Connell, "Industry-University Partnerships in the Curriculum: Trends and Developments in the OECD Countries", in *Industry and Higher Education*, (Feb 1996) pp. 9–22.

[8] Coolahan, J, *Irish Education: History and Structure* (Dublin: Institute of Public Administration) 1981.

[9] Smith, A and F Webster (eds), *The Postmodern University? Contested Visions of Higher Education in Society* (Buckingham: Society for Research into Higher Education and Open University Press) 1997.

very rapid. There is an extensive literature on issues in this debate, much of which has many points of relevance to developments in Ireland.[10]

Until the end of World War II, the universities were the principal higher education institutions in Ireland, and in common with those elsewhere, could be characterised as elite self-governing communities of learning. Academic self-government within these institutions comprised:

- the appointment and advancement of staff and the definition of their terms of employment

- the recruitment of students and the determination of the selection criteria

- the design and implementation of study programmes including deciding the subjects and curricula of courses

- the pursuit of research and the selection of the subject matter of the research carried out

- the setting of standards in courses and research studies

- the acquisition of new accommodation

- the buying and selling of land and other resources

- the spending of income from whatever sources.

A key concept encompassed in this self-governance was academic freedom, that is, the freedom of the institution to decide on its academic priorities and subjects for study, coupled with the freedom of the individual academic staff members to research and/or teach material and interpretations as they saw fit, with little regard to external pressures or authorities. Of course such academic freedom was never absolute. Each individual, and indeed each institution, was affected positively or negatively by the general environment and could be moulded by public opinion and other influences. A major democratic deficit in the academic freedom of higher education institutions has always been that while it may have applied to various extents to those within the institutions, it did not apply to the rest of the citizens in society, the great majority of whom had no access to them. Academic freedom was always a remarkably elite and exclusive concept.

Government involvement in funding and shaping higher education institutions dates from the middle of the 19th century in the United States.[11] There, many states established public land-grant universities to provide "an instrument of service throughout the state and a source of expert advice to its

[10]Barnett, R, *Higher Education: A Critical Business* (Buckingham: Society for Research into Higher Education and Open University Press) 1997.

[11]Melody, W, *Universities and Public Policy*, in Smith, A and F Webster, *op. cit.*

legislature".[12] These have developed into the huge state universities of today. While clearly regarded by the state governments as instruments of public policy and never as havens of disinterested learning, they gained wide popularity as they came to be viewed as agents for improving the economy and their degree awards came to provide access to good employment opportunities. In the period during and after World War II, both federal and local state governments, as well as industry, began funding huge research programmes in areas of science and technology in the universities. Beginning in the 1960s, their research programmes began to diversify significantly into other areas including the social sciences. These major financial contributions from government and industry transformed the nature and role of these universities. In the words of Bok, a former president of Harvard University, "as society came to rely more and more on universities, universities in turn grew more dependent on society for the money required to support their expanding activities". During the 1960s and early 1970s however, the universities provided a massive arena of opposition to the government's prosecution of the Vietnam War. Not surprisingly, according to Bok, "by 1975, the federal government was beginning to move on many fronts to regulate academic policies in ways that would bring them into closer conformity with national needs".

In Britain, the 1963 report of the Committee on Higher Education, also called the Robbins Report, overtly tied the development of the universities to the implementation of government policy.[13] The expansion of the universities had occurred broadly in parallel with the welfare state, and indeed as public institutions of the welfare state. Throughout this growth the government did not appreciably intervene in the internal life and governance of the universities and colleges of higher education.[14] However, since 1992 when some thirty-four polytechnics and other institutions were converted overnight into universities, higher education in Britain has undergone a major reorientation. In particular the government there has imposed a comprehensive system of institutional quality evaluation, which is outlined in Chapter 3, in relation to teaching and research in the higher education institutions.

Since 1972, the government in Ireland has used the National Council for Educational Awards to exert some external regulation on the former Regional Technical Colleges (now Institutes of Technology) but only recently made some moves to modify the governance of the universities, under the guidance of the HEA, with the enactment of the 1997 Universities Act. The

---

[12]Bok, D, *Beyond the Ivory Tower: Social Responsibilities of the Modern University* (Cambridge, MA: Harvard University Press) 1982.

[13]Committee on Higher Education, Cmnd 2154, *Higher Education* (London: HMSO) 1963.

[14]Throw, M, *Managerialism and the Academic Profession: The Case of England, The Quality Debate*, Times Education Supplement Seminar (Milton Keynes) 1993.

Qualifications (Education and Training) Act 1999 is aimed at copper-fastening this process in relation to the Institutes of Technology.

In the context of increasing its funding for the higher education institutions, the government in Ireland has begun to emphasise the need for the institutions to deliver value for money and in this respect to be more accountable. The government has not yet defined clearly what constitutes value for money or accountability. Whatever definitions emerge, they are virtually certain to place restrictions on institutional autonomy and academic freedom.

In moulding the institutions to provide improved service to society, still wider layers of society can benefit. But in the process it would be desirable that the individual commitment and creativity of each member of staff should not be compromised.

The reorientation of academic disciplines towards a more vocational or applied direction, such as applied sciences, technologies and the social sciences, and the increasing numbers attending the universities and other higher education institutions, have ensured that their nature and role are now in flux, both in Ireland and internationally. The governance of the institutions is changing to reflect the new reality. There is considerable literature on the need for a new model of the university, defined by a new and more flexible relationship with society, with individual citizens, with industry and with government.[15]

Universities, through their power to confer degrees, have long acted as gatekeepers to the professions and to a wide range of skilled employment opportunities in society. A degree tended to be a passport to permanent well paid employment. With the greater numbers participating in higher education and obtaining degree qualifications, this is now less often the case. Estimates vary as to the effective half life of the knowledge, skills and competencies acquired in a degree course, but there is little dispute, in this era of volatile technological and societal change, that the value of these knowledge, skills and competencies may not last a career time. In the context of all disciplines being shaped and reshaped and occasionally obliterated by new developments, some professions are becoming less relevant and new ones are being created before our eyes.

Consequently there is increasing emphasis on developing in undergraduates the necessary research and studying skills required to sustain a commitment to lifelong learning and constant re-education and retraining throughout one's career.

---

[15] Industrial Policy Review Group, *A Time for Change: Industrial Policy for the 1990s* (Baile Átha Cliath: Oifig an tSoláthair) 1992.

QUALITY IN HIGHER EDUCATION

Within this context of expansion and change, issues of academic quality have come to the fore internationally. In the event, many of the problems of comparability of standards and strategic planning in higher education have been revealed and are being investigated under the general banner of quality assurance and improvement. This book seeks to describe the emergence of quality assurance in higher education both internationally and in Ireland and considers the issues that have arisen in that process.

CHAPTER TWO

The Processes of Teaching, Research and Learning

The purpose of higher education, at the most general level, is to achieve effective learning or advanced knowledge acquisition by students through a variety of activities. Some of these are encompassed in the functions of the teachers, some in the functioning of the institution and others in the actions of the students themselves. The higher education institution provides the environment and the means for these activities and processes to occur effectively. Increasingly, modern telecommunications and information technology are playing a major role in these activities. The interaction between teachers and students is complex, but its fundamental aim is to provide the most effective teaching and learning possible. Since teaching without learning would be pointless, evaluating or working to improve teaching in isolation from learning would also be pointless.

Quality assurance procedures, therefore, must engage with these complex questions in relation to the nature of effective teaching and learning in higher education. How learning and teaching processes might be measured and assessed, particularly in this time of rapid technological, economic and social change, is the subject of this chapter.[1]

LEARNING IN HIGHER EDUCATION

Since the facilitation of learning is the purpose of teaching, it is worthwhile to consider the nature of learning in higher education. Following Brown, Figure 2.1 is a schematic model of student learning, where the learning process which prepares the student to make informed judgement, perform particular skilled actions and engage in creative activity, is affected by various preconditioning of the student and by the teaching processes. The student enters the learning process with certain knowledge, skills and mental attitudes.They are presented with a range of challenges and tasks to be actively undertaken and the interaction of the old and the new result in new knowledge, skill and competencies.

---

[1] Brown, G, "Effective Teaching" in Ellis, R (ed), *Quality Assurance for University Teaching* (Buckingham: Society for Research into Higher Education) 1993.

The model may include more specific student goals such as passing examinations and practical and course work assessments and may also incorporate different course designs, modes of teaching and procedures for assessment. It also provides for the possibility that learning can happen in the absence of teaching and the teacher.

Figure 2.1 Schematic model of student cognitive learning processes

1. Starting point
    (a) Previous knowledge *(facts, concepts, images, networks, orientation, links, maps)*
    (b) Intentions, motivation, study skills, personal context
    (c) Self-perception, task-perception, awareness of learning
    (d) Preferred/required orientation to learning *(knowledge-seeking, understanding-seeking)*
2. Active selection of old learning
3. Active processing *(linking, relating, structuring, re-structuring, adding, collecting, adapting, applying, refining, automating, memorising, analysing, synthesising, comparing, evaluating, imaging, problem-solving, sense-making)*
4. Active filtering and selection of new learning
    (a) New knowledge to be acquired *(new links, networks, relationships to be understood)*
    (b) Environment, general context

ORIENTATIONS TO LEARNING

Two principal orientations to learning have been described in the literature and summarised by Entwhistle.[2] These are the knowledge-seeking and understanding-seeking orientations.

In the knowledge-seeking orientation to learning, the student's approach is characterised by adding facts and information, collecting procedures and skills, breaking down tasks and problems into separate sub-units, making links within units of knowledge, memorising, working methodically and logically through problems, analysing, using a systematic trial and error approach

---

[2] Entwhistle, N, *Styles of Learning* (Chichester: John Wiley and Sons) 2nd edition, 1988.

and evaluating data. Multiple choice and other forms of examinations may be appropriate for assessing this type of learning.

In the understanding-seeking orientation to learning, the student or learner tries to relate information or tasks to their own experience, makes links with other bodies of knowledge, restructures information for their own personal meaning, synthesises, likes to work from the complete context, searches for underlying structure, purpose and meaning, uses knowledge intuitively, uses analogies and metaphors and tends to be independent and creative. Project work and more open-ended assessments tend to promote this orientation to learning.

The understanding-seeking orientation to learning tends to be more intellectually deep and independent than the knowledge-seeking approach, but the appropriateness of the orientation can depend strongly on the nature of the subject or discipline. Entwhistle and Tait have found that departments that promote the understanding-seeking orientation to learning tend to be perceived by students as being good teaching departments while the reverse is perceived of departments that primarily promote knowledge-seeking learning.[3]

TEACHING

Teaching in higher education encompasses the following activities:

- course design and specification

- course and resource management

- preparation of teaching and student material

- lecturing, teaching and tutoring

- assessment, including drafting examination papers, marking scripts, oral examining, report and thesis evaluation

- providing feedback and advice to students, including career counselling

- supervision of practical, workshop and studio work, including research project work

- dissertation and thesis review and editing

- provision and supervision of other learning opportunities such as professional practice, work placement and others

- collaborating with teams of colleagues in all of these activities.

---

[3] Entwhistle, N and H Tait, "Approaches to Learning, Evaluation of Teaching and Preferences for Contrasting Academic Environments", *Higher Education* (1990) No. 19, pp.169–194.

Any evaluation of the teaching process must take account of it as a multi-faceted activity with a range of depths of interaction between teacher and student. Any conception that only the face-to-face aspects of teaching need be evaluated would be seriously flawed.

The various methods of teaching may be viewed on a broad continuum from lecturing, small group tutoring, research supervision and laboratory supervision, to self-instruction and private study. At one extreme, in the lecture, student control and participation are minimal while the involvement of the teacher is greatest. Nevertheless the student can decide on the form of notes to take and on whether or not to ask questions. At the other extreme, in private study, teacher involvement tends to be minimal while that of the student tends to be greatest. Even in this case the teacher may be involved in aspects such as designing the course and prescribing textbooks. At other points along the continuum, the extent of teacher and student interaction can vary widely.

SKILLS OF TEACHING

Teaching requires the teacher to possess a range of interactive skills, describing, explaining, questioning, listening, responding to students' questions, comments and answers, assessing, giving guidance and feedback and, indeed, monitoring and improving the teaching process. Each of these skills is complex and any individual teacher generally will have different levels of competence in each of them.

The individual teacher's range of skills and their exploitation and development of them help to determine their style. One teacher's style may be well matched to face-to-face teaching of large or small groups but poorly suited to laboratory or project supervision. In any academic department, therefore, it is a key task of management to make these evaluations, to develop the best teaching team and to optimise the match between the teachers' teaching skills and the teaching needs of the course and department.

LECTURING

Lecturing is most pointedly an individual performance by the teacher. Possibly the key objective of lecturing is to provide information which will stimulate and encourage students to become active learners in their own right, if for no other reason than that no lecture or course of lectures can cover all aspects of a subject or discipline. The nature and style of lecturing are strongly related to the discipline and conditioned by the tools and aids used. However, there are features generally prized in good lecturing. These include clarity of concepts and content; the use of overall structure and signposts; engagement with the audience; summarising statements; examples, explanations, metaphors and interest (exemplified by insights, historical and other perspectives); emphasis on synthesising principles rather than minor details; responsiveness to students' queries and comments; the teacher's love or dislike for the subject; the teacher's preparedness for the lecture and the use of a searching, developmental approach rather than a dogmatic one.

SMALL GROUP TUTORING

Small group teaching or tutoring has a greatly increased continuous involvement by the students and is thought to be effective at promoting intellectual and discussion skills and helping to resolve individual students' difficulties. It is more labour-intensive and expensive than lecturing, but tends to involve all of the students in the group and to stimulate peer group teaching and greater individual student responsibility for their own learning. In this form of teaching, the teacher needs particular questioning, probing, listening and responding skills.

LABORATORY, WORKSHOP AND STUDIO SUPERVISION

Most generally associated with scientific, technological and other practical disciplines, laboratory teaching aims to teach manual, technical and observational skills, develop understanding of the methods of scientific inquiry and problem-solving, provide training in reporting such work in oral and written forms and generally develop professional approaches and attitudes to the discipline. Practice and feedback over time are key to laboratory supervision skills.

Frequently, good laboratory teaching alone may not contribute appreciably to developing understanding, although feedback on laboratory reports can help in this regard. In order to optimise the development of understanding and the learning of methods of inquiry, it is desirable that students' understanding of basic concepts and laboratory skills be developed in a progressive manner and be requisite to the tasks at hand at each stage. Preparatory teaching of these elements by other means is also required and indeed the laboratory experience itself should exemplify the scientific mode of inquiry, rather than be merely a procedure by recipe.

Brown, cited earlier, has listed the basic skills of laboratory teaching as:

- explaining and presenting information
- questioning, listening and responding
- giving directions

- teaching demonstrators
- helping technicians
- preparing a laboratory course.

An area of particular significance in laboratory teaching is project work, most typically on the final year project, especially in science and technology disciplines. The final year project is an introduction to research skills in the particular discipline and provides an opportunity to integrate a number of different strands of the overall course. The student may work independently or collaboratively in a team and gains experience in project planning, time management, both oral and written presentation skills, laboratory or other practical work, library research, and negotiation and other interactions with a supervisor.

The attributes of good project supervision include those for good laboratory teaching and others, such as:

- clarity of aims and assessment criteria
- clarity on length and format of oral and written reports
- provision of adequate resources
- timely and helpful interaction with the student(s)
- freedom for student(s) to work independently.

RESEARCH SUPERVISION

Supervision of research students, normally at the postgraduate level, is treated in some detail in Chapters 7 and 8. It involves many of those skills required for face-to-face and laboratory teaching, together with additional attributes. Based on the person-to-person interaction between teacher and student, research supervision has been receiving increased critical attention and analysis in recent years and requires skills of:

- project planning and structuring, including financial and time management, as well as establishing critical points and goals
- appraising the strengths and weaknesses of the student and arranging requisite training and learning
- induction and integration of the postgraduate student into a research group
- regular review of the progress of the work with the student
- careful and critical feedback on progress
- continuously moving the work forward

- academic and personal guidance

- support and encouragement

- drawing up theoretical and practical alternatives during the progress of the work

- commenting on oral presentations of the work

- editing and critically commenting on the draft thesis and on any draft joint publications.[4]

EFFECTIVENESS OF TEACHING

Any measure of quality or effectiveness in teaching must have declared learning outcomes and must show how well those goals are, in general, achieved. The complex nature of teaching means that any such measures will depend on the values, status, purpose and context of the assessor. Certainly any assessment that concentrates on lecturing alone can not capture the full range of dimensions of teaching. Expertise in lecturing does not imply expertise in small group teaching or in laboratory or research work. The reverse also holds true and it does not follow that a high quality researcher will automatically be a good lecturer or laboratory teacher. The value system of an institution, faculty or department must also be taken into account in evaluating any of these teaching activities. This value system, which should be formally stated, includes what the institution, department or teacher wants the students to learn; what the students actually do learn; how the institution or teacher teaches and how these things can be measured.

EVALUATION OF TEACHING AND RESEARCH

Processes as complex and multi-dimensional as teaching, learning and research may not be readily evaluated on a simple continuous scale. They can, at best, be evaluated on qualitative, comparative scales. In each case the evaluation seeks to determine the added value, the change between the beginning student with their knowledge, skills and competencies and the output graduate with their enhanced and broadened knowledge, skills and competencies, taking into account the cost of the process.

In the Republic of Ireland, the main stream of students beginning in the

---

[4] Cryer, P, *The Research Student's Guide to Success* (Buckingham: Open University Press) 1996; *Guidelines on the Quality Assurance of Research Degrees* (London: Higher Education Quality Council) 1996; Delamont, S, P Atkinson and O Parry, *Supervising the PhD* (Buckingham: Open University Press) 1997.

higher educational institutions consists of a section of the age cohort which in any year takes the national Leaving Certificate examination. In the case of any course, the incoming students possess a range of points, awarded according to performances in six subjects in the Leaving Certificate. The intake to any course, therefore, is not uniform and does not have a single starting point of previous knowledge, skills and competencies. The output of the course consists of the graduates with their range of certificate, diploma or degree performances and grades, who proceed to obtain employment, develop careers and perform and contribute as citizens and economic producers for the next forty years or more of their careers. The output graduates are far from uniform and the full value added in their education may not be fully apparent for many years. Therefore the appropriateness of quantitative evaluation at the output point is likely to be limited.

The intake to postgraduate research programmes may also be non-uniform, although much less than for undergraduate courses. This is because a high honours degree performance in a discipline related to the subject matter of the research is usually a prerequisite for acceptance into such a programme. The value added in postgraduate research also leads to a graduate with enhanced capacity to contribute to industry, business and society over her/his career. The quality of the research done in adding this value may also be qualitatively gauged, as outlined in Chapter 8, from the output of the research, the products produced and the publications or exhibitions resulting from the work.

SUMMARY

The inter-linked academic processes of teaching and learning in higher education are complex and multi-dimensional. They are not easily susceptible of quantitative measurement. Nevertheless a range of procedures, based fundamentally on steadily expanding and deepening the application of peer review, have been developed and accepted across the world and allow useful comparison between the teaching and learning achievement and quality in different institutions. These procedures, outlined in this book, also provide reliable pointers as to how academic quality can be improved and enhanced over time.

CHAPTER THREE

The Development of Quality Assurance in Higher Education

The methods and language of quality assurance, quality improvement and enhancement and quality audit, pioneered in industry and business, have been applied to higher education in many countries across the world over the past fifteen to twenty years.[1] In many respects these processes have been modern manifestations of the historical concern of the higher education institutions to achieve high academic standards. But the modern context gives them a special relevance and significance.

In the dramatic transformations underway in higher education in recent decades, quality assurance has been a key process in many countries, at times a test of the transformations and at other times a motor driving them forward.[2] This chapter reviews the broad international developments in this field.

DEVELOPMENTS IN BRITAIN

Higher education in England and Wales is now provided mainly by the 130 publicly funded universities and colleges.[3] There are 46 pre-1992 universities, 34 post-1992 universities (most of which had been polytechnics) and 50 colleges. These institutions are autonomous, each being responsible for its own academic, administrative and financial management. Universities award their own degrees, while most colleges award degrees validated by universities. Generally, courses leading to primary degrees take three years of full time

---

[1] Deming, W E, *Quality, Productivity and Competitive Position* (Cambridge, MA: MIT Press) 1982; Crosby, P, *Quality without Tears* (New York: McGraw-Hill) 1984; International Organisation for Standardisation, Case Postale 56, CH-1211, (Genève, Switzerland); Australian Quality Council, *Program of Courses* (St. Leonards, NSW, Australia) 1995.

[2] Ellis, R, "Quality Assurance for University Teaching: Issues and Approaches" in Ellis, R (ed), *Quality Assurance for University Teaching* (Buckingham: Society for Research into Higher Education) 1993.

[3] OECD, *Education at a Glance* (Paris) 1995 pp. 312–314; "Higher Education Systems in the European Union Member States: Background Note", *Vocational Training European Journal* (1997) No. 10.

study, or correspondingly longer on a part time basis. Shorter undergraduate courses lead to diploma awards. Postgraduate courses, usually of one year's duration, lead to master's degrees while master's degrees by research and doctoral qualifications require at least one and a half and over three years of postgraduate study and research respectively.

The need for appraisal of teaching and research performance, driven by government concerns in relation to transparency, efficiency and value for public money, has been a particularly strong feature of higher education developments in Britain.[4]

Before World War II the universities in Britain received about one third of their income directly from central government, the remainder coming from tuition fees, local government grants and endowments in land and investments. This funding structure gave the universities considerable autonomy relative to the government and this autonomy was enshrined in their royal charters.

The government in 1919 established the University Grants Committee (UGC) as the agency for the allocation of central government funds, as block grants, to the universities. This agency did not interfere in the internal governance or operation of the universities, even in the period after World War II when the funding allocated increased considerably. This system of university funding continued until 1991, long after the Thatcher government of the previous decade had called into question the universities' right to an annual blank cheque from the government, regardless of the performance of the individual institutions.

Each university was traditionally free to devise its own approach and procedures for the assurance of academic standards. It selected its staff and students using its own conditions and criteria, designed its own programmes and curricula and awarded its own degrees. There was very little questioning of academic quality. Rather, the broad working assumption was that, if they had equals, they had no peers in the world.

Probably the most generally used instrument of what is now seen to be quality assurance was the system of external examiners. The external exam-

---

[4] Sterian, P E, *Accreditation and Quality Assurance in Higher Education*, Papers on Higher Education, CEPES (UNESCO) 1992, pp. 21–23; van Vught, F A and D F Westerheijden, *Quality Management and Quality Assurance in European Higher Education: Methods and Mechanisms*, Center for Higher Education Policy Studies, University of Twente, 1993, pp. 17–20; European Commission, *Socrates: European Pilot Project for Evaluating Quality in Higher Education*, European Report (Brussels) 1995, pp. 52–53; Committee of University Chairmen *Guide for Members of Governing Bodies of Universities and Colleges in England and Wales* (London) 1995; OECD, *Universities under Scrutiny* (Paris) 1987; Magennis, S, "Appraisal Schemes and their Contribution to Quality in Teaching" in Ellis, R (ed), *op. cit*; Levy, J, "Engineering Education in the United Kingdom: Standards, Quality Assurance and Accreditation", *Int. J. Engng. Ed.*, 16(2), 136–145, 2000.

iner was usually an eminent academic in the discipline of the programme, but from an external higher education institution or occasionally from industry. Such examiners reviewed examination papers and the students' examination scripts and other work, to assess principally whether it was of a standard comparable to that of students at the same stage elsewhere in the country and internationally.

In some disciplines accreditation by a professional body, usually involving a periodic assessment visit by a visiting committee from the professional body, also provided a substantial element of quality assurance. The graduates of an accredited programme were typically exempt from various professional examinations required for membership of the professional body.

In general, however, the academic and professional authority of the professor, as academic leader and chairperson of the discipline-based department, underpinned the standards of courses and other programmes provided by a department.

The development of the welfare state in the United Kingdom after World War II saw the government increase its funding to the universities and other higher education institutions. In 1963, the Colleges of Advanced Technology were designated as universities, intended, initially at least, to cater mostly for science and technology disciplines.

Beginning in the mid-1960s a number of other higher education institutions came to be designated as polytechnics and a national system of quality management was applied to this non-university sector in Britain. This system was co-ordinated through the Council of National Academic Awards (CNAA) which received its charter in 1964 as a degree-awarding body. Although established by the government, it functioned relatively independently.

The CNAA carried out its quality management role by validating proposed programmes of study in polytechnics and colleges in advance of their delivery, approving the appointment of external examiners and reviewing the programmes on a five-yearly cycle thereafter. A validation committee, consisting of a number of academics in the same discipline but from external higher education institutions and a number of industrial and/or professional experts in the discipline, visited the institution. In preparation for the visit, the validation committee was supplied with detailed documentation on the structure and content of the proposed programme of study, the methods of teaching, learning and assessment, the resources available to run the programme and the staff academic profile. The validation committee submitted a written report following the institutional visit, either approving or disapproving of the validation of the programme. In the event of disapproval, the report would normally outline the weaknesses in the proposal and provide recommendations for a later resubmission. Frequently, in the event of approval, some recommendations were made and conditions of approval stipulated.

The five-yearly reviews of programmes followed a procedure very similar to the initial validation procedure.

Within the CNAA mechanisms, as well as the programme validation and five-yearly reviews, there was also a five-yearly review or audit of each institution's operational quality assurance procedures. This type of review, based principally on self-assessment by the institution itself, dealt with the institution's procedures for annual internal reporting on and improvement of programmes, its response to external examiners' recommendations and the development and publishing of performance indicators.

Following the 1988 Education Reform Act, the CNAA used this institutional self-assessment to accredit some polytechnics and give them authority to validate their own programmes for primary and postgraduate degree awards. Also, together with the Polytechnics and Colleges Funding Council (PCFC), the CNAA began to take account of each institution's own mission and goals in making the institutional assessment. In this way each institution was given much more autonomy than had been possible in the earlier more centralised CNAA system.

During this period, Her Majesty's Inspectorate (HMI) also had a quality management role in parallel with the CNAA, especially in relation to classroom observation of the teaching process. HMI assessments were, for instance, a factor in the funding allocations made by the PCFC.

The CNAA was discontinued with the implementation of the 1992 Further and Higher Education Act.

There were major cuts in government funding to the universities in the early 1980s. The tone of the Conservative government's attitude to higher education was encapsulated in the notion that the principal objectives for higher education should be quality and value for money. Largely in response to the funding crisis, the Committee of Vice-Chancellors and Principals (CVCP), the umbrella organisation of the universities, set up the Steering Committee for Efficiency Studies in the Universities to report on efficiency and accountability in the universities. The resulting report, the Jarratt Report of 1985, named after the chairperson of the Steering Committee, began the process of introducing transparent procedures for planning, resource allocation and accountability as parts of the corporate process within the universities.[5] This report also introduced the language and methods of business and finance into university governance. In its aftermath, vice-chancellors became chief executives and more overt management layers were developed below them down to departmental level. Quantitative and qualitative measures that came to be called performance indicators were developed to indicate levels of performance and accountability. One such indicator was the annual appraisal

---

[5] Jarratt, S A, *Report of the Steering Committee for Efficiency Studies in Universities*, Committee of Vice-Chancellors and Principals (CVCP) of the Universities of the United Kingdom (London) 1985.

of staff members, which became a feature of university life after 1986.[6]

In the period to 1992 each university determined its own quality assurance procedures. By that time it was beginning to emerge that this might not be an adequate measure of accountability, when viewed by government as the principal funding agency, or indeed by society in general. The conversion of the polytechnics, which had been under the aegis of the CNAA, to universities, was a major influence in changing this situation. In order to maintain overall university control over quality assurance in the universities, the CVCP established an Academic Audit Unit (AAU) in 1990.

The AAU operated on three tracks — quality assurance procedures similar to those of the CNAA, financial audits and total quality management assessment. The financial audit entailed an external review of the institution's financial accounting systems and included a detailed examination of how some of them operated in practice. The total quality management assessment involved a review of the institution's academic quality assurance system and procedures and also included a detailed examination of some of them in actual operation. The AAU developed a benchmark checklist based on best practice against which the institution's procedures were compared. This checklist contained guidelines on matters such as curriculum organisation and planning, staff academic profile, methods of teaching, learning and assessment, reports and recommendations of external examiners and feedback from students.

These AAU assessments did not evaluate the quality of the institution's programmes but rather the quality of the institution's own evaluation procedures. They directed attention to aspects that previously had received little attention in higher education, such as student satisfaction, staff training and development for quality improvement and the dependence of the academic quality of programmes on the rest of the institution's activities.

The AAU quality assessment procedure consisted mainly of a three-day visit to the institution by an audit team. This audit team normally consisted of two or three academics. The visit was by invitation from the institution, usually after a discussion between the AAU and the institution. In advance of the visit the audit team was supplied by the institution with a written report on the quality assessment systems, giving some examples of their operation. This documentation, together with the AAU checklist and the information gathered during the institutional visit, became the basis of the report drafted by the audit team. This draft report was submitted to the institution as a whole, occasionally with a confidential report on sensitive issues to the vice-chancellor or chief officer. The institution made comments on the draft report, following which an official report was written and submitted to the institution.

---

[6] Magennis, S, *op. cit.*; Thackwray, B and H Hamblin, "Total Quality Management, Investors in People and Higher Education", *Engineering Science and Education Journal* (June 1996) pp.113–119.

The institution was encouraged to publish this report, but the AAU did not do so.

The Further and Higher Education Act 1992 gave rise to a range of major changes in the organisation of the higher education system itself and the quality assurance systems operating within it. The heads of the institutions established the Higher Education Quality Council (HEQC), which was entrusted with the application and extension of the work of the CNAA and the AAU in relation to quality improvement across the full spectrum of higher education institutions. The HEQC established a Division of Quality Audit (DQA) and the AAU was subsumed within it. The two former funding councils, the UGC for the universities and the PCFC for the polytechnics, were reorganised into three new funding councils, one each for England, Scotland and Wales. Each of these has established a Quality Assessment Committee to facilitate decision making in relation to funding, based on teaching and learning quality in the individual institutions. In Northern Ireland the quality assessment task is carried out by the Department of Education for Northern Ireland (DENI).

In this system, the HEQC carries out a quality audit in a manner very similar to the AAU, to provide guarantees that the institution has suitable academic quality assurance mechanisms in place. Subsequently, the relevant funding council carries out an external assessment of the quality of the teaching and learning in the institution and this is a determinant in the funding allocation to that institution. Thus two separate and independent agencies carry out these separate functions.

During 1991 and 1992 a pilot project under the aegis of the Higher Education Funding Council for England (HEFCE), the HMI and the joint organisation of the higher education institutions, was carried out in order to develop the quality assessment procedure. A seven-person assessment team consisting of four academic peers, two representatives of the HMI and one non-academic chairperson was constituted as an inspection group. The group visited the test institutions participating in the pilot for one week, in order to inspect the resources and accommodation, view a selection of the lecturers at work and review a selection of the work of the students. By the end of 1992, and on the basis of the pilot project, the HEFCE had agreed upon a quality assessment procedure. In this, the institution or a faculty within it is required to provide information on its staff and programmes in terms of a number of indicators and to claim for themselves an "excellent" or "satisfactory" quality of teaching. The HEFCE then forms small visiting committees, composed of peers from the relevant discipline(s) drawn from a pool of experts, to visit and assess each institution claiming an "excellent" rating and also to visit a selection of other institutions. Each visiting committee visits one institution only and no effort is made to develop a national cross-comparison network. The only outcome of the quality assessment is that institutions are graded with one of the ratings, "excellent", "satisfactory" or "unsatisfactory".

The HEQC quality audit procedures have, as outlined above, developed logically from the CNAA and CVCP practices and are detailed in the handbooks, *Guidelines on Quality Assurance* and *Guidelines on the Quality Assurance of Research Degrees*.[7]

Some three months before the audit visit, the institution submits a range of specified briefing documentation to the Division of Quality Audit (DQA) of the HEQC. The briefing documentation from the institution is required to include the following elements:

- a formal statement of its aims, objectives and mission

- an outline of its academic strategic plan

- a description of the quality assurance procedures, with examples of relevant documentation on programmes

- the courses and programmes offered

- the management and organisational structure

- statistical information about the student body

- the policy documents relating to quality assurance

- staff recruitment and development procedures

- other relevant documentary information.

The audit team normally has three members ("auditors"), selected by the DQA, and an audit secretary. It meets about ten weeks in advance of the audit visit, to consider the briefing documentation in detail in the context of the following questions:

- What is the institution trying to do?

- Why is it trying to do it?

- How is it doing it?

- Why is it doing it that way?

- Why does it think that is the best way of doing it?

- How does it know it works?

- How does it improve it?[8]

---

[7] Higher Education Quality Council, *Guidelines on Quality Assurance* (London) 1996; Higher Education Quality Council, *Guidelines on the Quality Assurance of Research Degrees* (London) 1996.

[8] Higher Education Quality Council, *Notes for the Guidance of Auditors* (London) 1995.

The audit visit normally extends over three days. The audit team meets a full range of staff at all levels and groups of students, including student representatives, in order to probe issues raised in the briefing documentation and any others that arise. The report of the audit team on the visit provides an account of the institution's quality assurance system and procedures and a constructive and helpful analysis of their effectiveness and weaknesses.

In 1997 the Higher Education Quality Council (HEQC) was renamed the Quality Assurance Agency for Higher Education (QAAHE, or QAA for short).

The research assessment process in the universities in Britain and Northern Ireland was first undertaken in 1989 and repeated more recently in 1992 and 1996, under the aegis of the Higher Education Funding Councils for England (HEFCE), Scotland (SHEFC) and Wales (HEFCW) and the Department for Education in Northern Ireland (DENI). In this exercise the overall research effort in each university was rated on a five point comparative scale, expanded in 1996 to a seven-point scale. The seven point scale has the following seven qualitative grades of research quality:

5*   international level of excellence in most areas and national level of excellence in the other areas

5   international level of excellence in some areas and national level of excellence in most of the other areas

4   national level of excellence in most areas, possibly close to international level in some

3a   national level of excellence in large majority of areas

3b   national level of excellence in most areas

2   national level of excellence in up to half of the areas

1   national level of excellence in practically no area.

In order to make these comparative judgements, each discrete area or unit within the institution supplies information about their research promotion and management mechanisms. They also provide the following details:

• plans for future research

• numbers of staff engaged in the research effort

• numbers of postgraduate students

• numbers and financial amounts of research grants and contracts obtained and details of the funding agencies

• collaborations with external bodies, including international agencies

• numbers of doctorates and research masters' degrees awarded over the recent three years

- research publications and other accessible output — books, book chapters, refereed journal articles, conference contributions, other publications and exhibitions.

The research profile of each discrete unit, generally a discipline-based unit such as a department in an institution, is assessed by a panel which is formed by the funding councils and comprises specialist researchers, including members from overseas and from industry. Learned societies, professional bodies, business organisations and other interested bodies are invited to nominate members to the panels. The panel for the discipline or unit is constituted some nine months before the assessment date. Its composition and chairperson, and the criteria they are to use in the assessment are published some six months before the assessment. The assessments made by the panels are whether the research profile of the unit is of international level of excellence, of national level of excellence or of less than national level of excellence. Subsequently the assessments for all of the units in an institution are compiled and an overall research quality grade is computed for the institution as a whole.

The National Committee of Inquiry into Higher Education or the Dearing Committee, named after its chairperson, Prof. Ron Dearing, was appointed in 1996 by the British government to report and advise on the long-term development of higher education in Britain. Amongst the wide range of issues considered and recommendations made in the resulting Dearing Report were a number of quality assurance and quality audit matters.[9] Recommendations made in this context included the following:

- that institutions develop accredited programmes for teacher training of their staff and that institutions require all new full time academic staff with teaching responsibilities to achieve an appropriate teaching qualification

- that the remit of the QAA be amended to include quality assurance and public information, standards verification and the maintenance of a national qualifications framework

- that the QAA work with institutions to establish expert teams to provide benchmark information on standards, create a pool of academic staff from which institutions must select external examiners, develop a system for complaints relating to educational provision and review the arrangements for granting degree awarding powers

- that the Government enable the removal of degree awarding powers from an institution where the QAA demonstrates that the power to award degrees has been seriously abused

---

[9] Dearing, R, *Higher Education in the Learning Society,* Report of the National Committee of Inquiry into Higher Education (London) 1997.

- that the QAA ensures that its procedures and requirements do not discourage collaboration between institutions.

HOLLAND

Higher education in Holland has two strands, the university (WO) strand and the higher professional education (HBO) strand.[10] Until 1993 these two strands functioned under different legislation but the Higher Education and Research Act 1993 drew both strands together.

Admission to HBO colleges is open to those who have completed one of the three higher forms of secondary schooling, which are senior general secondary education (HAVO), pre-university education (VWO) and senior secondary vocational education (MBO). These colleges provide some courses of a bridging nature between secondary and tertiary levels but mainly practical and theoretical training for various applied disciplines. Their undergraduate courses last up to four years. Graduates have the title *ingenieur* (ing) or *baccalaureus* (bc). These colleges also provide some postgraduate (termed *"post-doctoraal"*) courses and may have limited research programmes that relate to the training courses provided.

Admission to WO universities requires a VWO certificate or equivalent. The universities provide undergraduate degree courses of up to four years' duration and primary degree graduates receive the title *doctorandus* (drs), *meester* (mr) or *ingenieur* (ir), depending on the discipline. The universities also provide postgraduate (*"post-doctoraal"*) academic training courses of one to four years' duration for what are termed trainee research assistants (AIO) and postgraduate vocational courses for doctors, dentists and veterinary surgeons. General pure and applied postgraduate research leading to postgraduate awards is also the responsibility of the universities.

In 1982 a quality assessment system for research was put in place by the Dutch government and was used for the assignment of research funding in the universities and other institutions of higher education.[11] In 1985 the government published a policy document, *"Higher Education: Autonomy*

---

[10] OECD, *Education at a Glance, op. cit.*, pp. 292–294; *Higher Education Systems in the European Union Member States, op. cit.*

[11] Sterian, P E, *op. cit.*, pp. 23–25; van Vught, F A and D F Westerheijden, *op. cit.*, pp. 14–17; Vroeijenstijn, A I, *Current Dutch Policy Towards Assessing Quality in Higher Education*, 5th Intl. Conference on Assessing Quality in Higher Education (Bonn) 1993; Vroeijenstijn, A I, *Methodology and Implementation of Quality Assurance in Higher Education — the Netherlands Experience*, Seminar on Self-Regulatory Approach to Quality Assurance in Dublin Institute of Technology (Dublin) 1994; European Commission, *Socrates: European Pilot Project for Evaluating Quality in Higher Education, op. cit.*, pp. 51–52.

and Quality", in order to restructure and define the relationship between the Department of Education and Science and the higher education institutions. This policy sought an arrangement whereby the institutions would be accorded an increased financial and managerial autonomy in exchange for an increased accountability in relation to the quality of the education they delivered.

The government established a Higher Education Inspectorate (IHO) to carry out the quality inspection and assessment. However, the organisation of the universities, the Association of Co-operating Universities in the Netherlands (VSNU) and the HBO Council decided to assume responsibility for quality assurance and assessment themselves. The IHO was left with responsibility for the evaluation of the assessments and the follow up of the assessments by the higher education institutions. In 1986 the government acquiesced in this arrangement and also agreed that the quality assessments would not be used as the basis for funding allocations to the institutions.

Following a pilot scheme in 1988, the VSNU quality assessment procedures came into operation in 1989 and a broadly similar scheme came into operation under the aegis of the HBO Council in 1990. In these schemes assessment of teaching is carried out separately from the assessment of research, although research evaluation is included in the assessment of teaching where it is related to teaching or underpins its quality, such as staff skills and training, environment and ethos. Since 1994, both teaching and research assessments have been carried out in parallel, but simultaneously, to allow faculties and departments to obtain a comprehensive overview of their activities and standards.

The VSNU system is funded and controlled fully by the combined universities. While the original intention of the government was to obtain a level of accountability in relation to academic quality, the emphasis that has been built into the system and accepted by the government, is one of quality improvement. In practice this means that, generally, the assessments give the institutions recommendations towards quality improvement rather than absolute evaluations of quality.

The system is discipline based, not institution based. A visiting committee assesses all the programmes in a discipline area in the country. Over a six-year period, all disciplines are assessed. The visiting committee has up to seven members. One member is a foreign expert in the relevant field who has knowledge of the Dutch language and higher education system. Another member is an educational expert. The expertise of the other members is required to broadly cover the main sub-sections of the discipline and they generally come from the relevant professions and from other sections of the Dutch higher education system. An independent chairperson is appointed. The deans of the faculties participating in the assessment propose members of the visiting committee, but the board of the VSNU decides its composition.

The visiting committee visits every centre offering a programme, each for two to three days. In advance of this visit, the staff members providing the programme carry out a self-evaluation or self-study, which not only serves as a preparation for the visit, but also facilitates internal quality improvement and allows particular strengths to be highlighted. The self-study report outlines the aims and objectives of the programme and describes in the main how it achieves these. A checklist of topics to be addressed in the self-study report is provided and these include factual information on the academic profile of staff, students, resources, administration and other institutional matters. The self-study reports from all the centres offering programmes in a discipline are submitted to the visiting committee before it embarks on the series of visits to the centres.

During the visit to the department in the institution, the visiting committee meets all the participants in the programme, academic and management staff and students. An open session is always part of the visit, so that any staff member or student may meet the visiting committee in a free atmosphere. The issues discussed during the visit are those arising from the self-study report, from earlier visits to other centres, from the expertise of the members of the visiting committee and from matters that emerge during the visit itself. At the end of the visit the chairperson provides an oral report on the assessment. Based on this oral report and the comments of the staff of the centre, the final written report of the visiting committee is later prepared, to formalise the visiting committee's assessment and recommendations on the quality of the programmes. This report normally contains a section that indicates problems, suggestions and recommendations relating to the overall discipline and specific chapters on the individual programmes in each centre.

The recommendations of the visiting committee, together with the measures taken during the internal self-evaluation in advance of the visit, are intended to lead to improvements in the quality of the programme. Institutional follow up is expected and has been found to occur to a limited extent.

The IHO reviews all these reports on behalf of the government and prepares an annual overall assessment report. The newspapers also give significant attention to these reports. While the Department of Education and Science has not used these quality assessment reports directly in its decisions about funding allocations, in recent years it has sought more detailed feedback from the universities on their follow-up measures.

Since 1995 the higher vocational education (HBO) sector has implemented an internal quality system adapted from the model of the European Foundation for Quality Management.[12] This model envisages nine functions and suggests that the *leadership* (function one) should provide guidance and content for *policy and strategy* (function two), *human resource management* (function three) and *physical resource management* (function four). These

---

[12]HBO Expert Group, *Method for the Improvement of the Quality of Higher Education in Accordance with the EFQM Model* (Gröningen) 1998.

are the organisational foundation and framework for implementing the *educational process management* (function five). In turn this determines *customer satisfaction* (function six), *people satisfaction* (function seven) and the *impact on society* (function eight), all three of which lead to the *overall business results* (function nine).

The approach in the model can be applied to a department, a faculty or an institution as a whole. Different specified attributes of each of the nine functional elements of the model can be scored on a quality scale ranging from one to five. Thus the current stage of development, for instance, of the *leadership* in relation to quality improvement would have a scale, calibrated relative to the leadership's activity (in brackets), thus:

1. (leaves quality to each member of staff)

2. (gives some encouragement to staff to improve quality)

3. (has formal consultation with staff to stimulate quality improvement)

4. (provides active guidance for quality improvement)

5. (is continuously engaged in improvement of quality).

Similar scales have been developed for each of the nine functions mentioned above. They allow the performance in quality improvement to be charted over time, particularly from one external audit to the next. External audits thus provide external calibration for the internal self-evaluations.

FRANCE

In France, higher education is provided by the universities, including the University Institutes of Technology (IUTs), the *grandes écoles*, third-level courses in certain *lycées*, the *écoles spécialisées*, the higher technician sections (STSs) and the *écoles d'architecture*.[13] Admission to higher education is generally through the achievement of the *baccalauréat* (general, technical or vocational) but the *grandes écoles* recruit through competitive examinations, often requiring up to two years post-*baccalauréat* study in a *lycée*.

The IUTs and STSs provide two-year courses leading to diplomas. The universities also award a diploma after two years of study. Primary degrees usually require three additional years of study, while after four additional years, master's degrees are awarded. Thus many primary degrees from universities and *grandes écoles* require five years of third level study. A

---

[13] OECD, *Education at a Glance, op. cit.*, pp. 273–275; *Higher Education Systems in the European Union Member States, op. cit.*

research doctorate or a degree in many medical disciplines requires up to nine or ten years, in total, of third level study.

The universities are state-funded but have had a significant level of autonomy since 1968.[14] The state reserves to itself the power to confer diplomas and degrees. Each higher education institution enters into a contract with the Department of Education every four years on its development programme. This programme covers all courses, research, physical and staff development and any special areas of service. Within this contract, budget allocations are made each year.

In order to reduce the rigidity and bureaucratic nature of the centralised system of quality control, the *Loi Savary* 1985 was enacted and through this the *Comité National d'Evaluation* (CNE) was established by the President of the Republic and an act of parliament. The CNE is a government agency that reports only to the President. Thus, to emphasise its objectivity, the CNE is independent of and does not report to the Department of Education or the *Premier*, and is also independent of the educational institutions that it assesses.

There are seventeen members of the CNE, who are appointed for four years by the President. Six members come from government agencies such as the *Conseil Economique et Social*, the *Conseil d'Etat* and the *Cour des Comptes*, while the remaining eleven come from the academic community, nominated by the universities and research organisations. The CNE carries out academic quality assessments of two types, discipline assessments and institutional assessments. It does not assess courses or programmes separately.

In the institutional assessment, the CNE evaluates quality within the general context of the operation of the four-year contract between the institution and the Department of Education. As well as issues such as academic programmes, research and staff and students, the institutional assessment also reviews accommodation and environment, financial management and general administration. This assessment is undertaken by the CNE, usually within a year after an invitation by the institution. Its timing therefore is at the discretion of the institution, but the CNE plans to carry out such an institutional assessment approximately once every eight years. The first round of these assessments was completed in 1992 with the second round to be completed by 2000. Each assessment report, with its recommendations, is submitted to the senior management of the institution, made public and also sent to the Department of Education. It therefore plays a role in the negotiations in preparation for the four-year contract between the institution and the Department. In these institutional reports, the CNE does not make quantitative evaluations of the quality and standards of the institutions and does not rank them.

---

[14]Sterian, P E, *op. cit.*, pp. 19–20; van Vught, F A and D F Westerheijden, *op. cit.*, pp. 13–14; European Commission, *Socrates: European Pilot Project for Evaluating Quality in Higher Education, op. cit.*, pp. 49–51.

The CNE discipline assessments cover all programmes in a broad discipline area. In preparation for such an assessment, a confidential self-evaluation report is first prepared by the staff of the department or discipline area of an institution. Then the CNE itself, each institution involved and the office of the Department of Education gather a range of statistical data concerning the discipline within the higher education sector and more generally. Finally a visiting committee is formed by the CNE to assess the self-evaluation reports from all the institutions and the data gathered on the discipline area, and then visit the institutions. This committee of external peers has between fifteen and twenty members, most of whom are from the academic community, two from industry and one a foreigner. After visiting the institutions, the visiting committee makes a qualitative, descriptive report. In the case of these discipline assessments, again the CNE does not rank the institutions.

DENMARK

Before the mid-1980s the higher education institutions in Denmark — thirteen universities and university level institutions and a number of other institutions involved mainly in medical and health areas — were, to an extent, centrally governed, with budgets allocated to individual faculties according to standard formulae.[15] The structure and academic content of each programme were controlled by the Department of Education and Research and in many disciplines student quotas were also centrally determined. The main quality assurance mechanism was the system of external examiners from an appointed national panel who participated in the examination processes.

A more extensive system of quality assurance was introduced in 1989 by the Committee of Chairpersons of the Danish Education Councils (CCDEC) in the social, natural and technical sciences.[16] Extensive evaluations of a limited range of disciplines in several institutions were carried out by the secretariat of the CCDEC. It became clear that a larger evaluating agency was required and, in 1991, the CCDEC and the Department of Education and Research agreed to establish an independent central evaluating agency for higher education. The national Centre for Quality Assurance and Evaluation of Higher Education (CQAEHE) was formed in 1992.

In 1990 the Minister of Education and Research had begun a series of higher education reforms to provide modular programmes with greater stu-

---

[15]OECD, *Education at a Glance, op. cit.*, pp. 267–269; *Higher Education Systems in the European Union Member States, op. cit.*

[16]Jensen, H P, "Quality Management: Danish Engineering Education", *Int. J. Engng. Ed.* 16(2), 127–135, 2000; European Commission, *Socrates: European Pilot Project for Evaluating Quality in Higher Education, op. cit.*, p. 49.

dent choice. The institutions were given greater freedom to determine which programmes they would offer and student quotas were removed in many disciplines. Improved student mobility between programmes and indeed between institutions began to exert a greater pressure for improved programmes and standards of teaching. There was, however, a fear that one way in which institutions might make their programmes more attractive to students would be to lower standards. This fear emphasised the need for a centralised system of programme evaluation.

Although accepted reluctantly by the rectors of the Danish universities, the CQAEHE was established by legislation. Its aims were to implement evaluation processes, develop mechanisms for programme assessment, provide guidance to institutions in respect of quality and evaluation and generally draw together a structure based on national and international practice. The Centre decided initially to concentrate on teaching programmes only, even though the institutions emphasised the symbiotic relationship between teaching and research. In fact a separation between the government's funding arrangements for teaching and research had already been established and a research evaluation process had been initiated. Then, in 1993, a new Department of Research and Technology was established and responsibility for research was separated from Education. The CQAEHE also decided at that stage that evaluations would be mandatory because of the growing need for comprehensive and systematic evaluations.

The programme of evaluations is seen by the CQAEHE as an incentive and a support to the institutions to develop their own processes of quality assurance and improvement. The Centre developed a five-year plan to complete a cycle of evaluations, by discipline, of the programmes in all the higher education institutions between 1993 and 1998. The five-year cycle is being repeated in the five-year period from 1998.

An Education Council, the Department of Education or the institution itself may request an evaluation. When requested, the Centre sets up a steering committee to oversee the evaluation and this committee has an authoritative and independent chairperson, at least two major employers of graduates from the programmes in the discipline and an appropriate number of other experts of standing and integrity. A secretariat is also appointed to the committee.

The institution carries out a comprehensive self-study under the guidance of the CQAEHE. The self-study documentation is required to provide details on the relevant programme(s), related postgraduate and other programmes, external links and collaborations, international study placements, practical training provided, student body profile, external examiners and special characteristics of the programme. The documentation is a blend of quantitative and qualitative information. The mechanism of self-study, including the preparation of the documentation, allows the institution to deepen its own process of quality assurance and improvement.

A team of three or four independent experts in the discipline, led by the chairperson of the steering committee, is formed by the Centre to consider the self-study documentation and to visit the institution. In its preparation for the visit, the team carries out surveys of the students on the study programme, recent graduates and employers of graduates in the private and public sectors. Reports from external examiners are also reviewed. When the steering committee's draft report is available, it is discussed with representatives of the institution. The report is then reviewed and finalised by the steering committee, which submits it to the Education Council and makes it available to the institution and to the public domain.

SWEDEN

In Sweden, higher education, divided into undergraduate studies and postgraduate studies and research, is provided in the universities.[17] All programmes of study have established curricula, with component courses having different durations. A student is free to choose his or her own study route and a primary degree can take from two to five years' study. Two years of postgraduate study lead to the award of *licenciat* and two further years of study are required for the award of *doktor.*

Admission to higher education requires a minimum of a pass in the three-year programmes of the upper secondary school (*gymnasieskolan*) system, but additional selection mechanisms are used including aptitude tests, interviews, work experience or previous education.

In the late 1980s, some steps towards greater autonomy of the institutions were implemented. These included a three-year instead of a one-year funding and budgeting cycle, a more general funding system allowing greater scope for local decision making and a majority of external representatives on governing bodies.[18] In return, the government sought some form of assessment of the academic standards and quality of the higher education institutions.

The unitary nature of the higher education system was reformed still more by the Higher Education Act of 1993 which gave much greater autonomy to the universities. While each institution was given greater control over the organisation and range of study programmes offered and the student was

---

[17] OECD, *Education at a Glance, op. cit.*, pp. 305–307; *Higher Education Systems in European Union Member States, op. cit.*

[18] Bauer, M, "Evaluation in Swedish Higher Education: Recent Trends and the Outlines of a Model", *European Journal of Education* (1988) No. 23, pp. 25-36; Sterian, P E, *op. cit.*, p. 25; National Agency for Higher Education, *The Current System of Quality Assurance in Sweden* (Stockholm) 1995.

accorded increased freedom of choice over their study route, the allocation of funding to each institution was made more dependent than previously on the numbers of students enrolled and on student performance.

The 1993 reforms also placed great emphasis on quality and quality enhancement in order to enable the Swedish universities to compete in the international educational market place and to participate actively in the development of the knowledge society. The primary responsibility for quality assurance was entrusted to the higher education institutions themselves and each was charged with preparing a programme of quality assurance that would be followed up and assessed.

The National Agency for Higher Education (*Högskoleverket or* NAHE), established as part of the reform process, formed the Office of the University Chancellors (*Kanslersämbetet*) to carry out institution-based, discipline-based and programme-based reviews of the monitoring, assessment and follow-up of quality assurance in the higher education system. Self-evaluation and self-regulation were the main elements of the assessment procedures developed.

The procedures for institution based quality assessments consist of three phases, data collection and self-evaluation, peer review and, some three to five years later, a follow up assessment of the results of the first two phases. The follow up assessment, carried out by the NAHE, is intended as an external impetus for the internal academic quality renewal and improvement. A visiting committee of external peers conducts the assessment, which first reviews the self-evaluation documentation from the institution and then visits the institution to evaluate the implementation of the quality assurance programmes. The visiting committee submits a report to the Office of the University Chancellors which, in turn, makes recommendations for improvements to the institution and to government. The first such assessments of quality assurance were carried out in 1994/1995 and it is planned that they be carried out in three-year cycles for each institution.

In parallel, the NAHE also carries out assessments of programmes, disciplines, departments and procedures (e.g. recruitment and registration and administration of examinations). It has responsibility for evaluating the quality of a discipline in an institution to determine whether it is qualified to award degrees of the various levels in that discipline. The Agency also has the task of granting the right to establish a professorship in a discipline in the institution, based on an evaluation of the academic environment, research facilities and ethos of that discipline in the institution.

GERMANY

The higher education sector in Germany comprises universities and other institutions including colleges of trade and technical subjects (*fachschulen*), health sciences, public administration and education and the higher vocational colleges *(fachhochschulen)*.[19] Only the universities are entitled to award doctorates. The higher vocational colleges offer highly applied courses, especially in science, technology and design, up to primary degree level. Such graduates must attend university to achieve postgraduate qualifications. The other colleges tend to offer advanced vocational courses, mostly of three years duration, but there are many avenues for horizontal transfer to colleges offering courses leading to higher qualifications.

In Germany responsibility for quality assurance in higher education rests at one level with the individual institution which determines its own standards and at another level with the local state government which determines the levels of equivalence between different courses and qualifications.[20] Thus the institution sets the standards of programmes, implements procedures to achieve them, evaluates the performance and results of the programmes and uses these evaluations to modify the conduct of the programmes. The state government in turn establishes general regulations on matters such as staff recruitment and promotion, examinations, student and staff mobility and in general ensures the broad comparability of courses and programmes.

External stakeholders, employers and the general public exert influence on academic quality through market mechanisms including employment of graduates and the popularity and uptake of courses.

There are, therefore, very few formal quality assurance or quality audit procedures or systems in place in Germany. However, since 1995, pilot studies have been conducted in a number of local government regions "on the evaluation in the field of higher education, with particular reference to the assessment of teaching" and an evaluation agency has been established in Lower Saxony.[21]

COUNCIL OF EUROPE

The Council of Europe was formed in 1949 as a political intergovernmental body, with terms of reference broadly to promote democracy, human rights and a European cultural identity. At the present time, 38 European countries are members. As long ago as 1959 it promulgated a convention on the mutual recognition of academic qualifications which was subscribed to over the next eight years by Austria, Belgium, Denmark, France, West Germany, Greece,

---

[19] OECD, *Education at a Glance, op. cit.*, pp. 276–278; *Higher Education Systems in the European Union Member States, op. cit.*

[20] Sterian, P E, *op. cit.*, pp. 20–21; Heitmann, G, "Quality Assurance in German Engineering Education against the Background of European Developments", *Int. J. Engng. Ed.*, 16(2), 117–126, 2000.

[21] European Commission, *Socrates: European Pilot Project for Evaluating Quality in Higher Education, op. cit.*, p. 16.

Iceland, Ireland, Italy, Luxembourg, Malta, the Netherlands, Norway, Sweden, Turkey and the United Kingdom.[22]

The Council has had a considerable involvement in academic quality assurance, assisting countries in Central and Eastern Europe with higher education reforms, but with a focus on legal, structural and organisational aspects of the higher education institutions. It has not been concerned with methodologies.[23]

EUROPEAN UNION

The Commission of the European Union (EU) has been active in relation to quality assurance in higher education along two broad strands — inter-university co-operation, including staff and student transfer in the EU and beyond, and developing procedures for evaluating academic quality.

The EU and its predecessors have promoted inter-institutional co-opera-tion, through student and staff interchange and collaborative research pro-grammes, for over thirty years. It aims to create an "open European area of higher education and training where students and teachers can move without obstacles".[24] A key element of this process is the development of the Euro-pean Credit Transfer System (ECTS). In this system students accumulate academic credits, based on their workload, for courses successfully taken in an institution. They may transfer these credits to other institutions, possibly in other countries, which have agreed to mutual recognition. In the system, the successful completion of a conventional full time student's annual work-load would earn 60 ECTS credits.

The system is founded on three elements thus:

- clear information being made available about the study programmes and the student's achievement

- mutual agreement between the partner institutions and the student

- use of ECTS credits to indicate the student's workload.

ECTS credits carry no connotation of the level or difficulty of an element of a course. For this reason transparent information about the course is essential for useful transfer of the credits gained. There is a grading scheme associated with ECTS, but its application is still being evaluated and developed.

---

[22]Council of Europe, *European Convention on the Academic Recognition of Univer-sity Qualifications* (Strasbourg) 1971.

[23]European Commission, *Socrates: Initiatives of Quality Assurance and Assessment of Higher Education in Europe* (Brussels) 1995.

[24]European Commission, *European Credit Transfer System, Users' Guide* (Brussels) 1995.

The use of ECTS credits by institutions is voluntary, but their use has helped to build links of trust and collaboration between institutions and to make wide choices available to students across Europe.

During the years 1994 and 1995 the Commission of the EU organised a major European pilot project for evaluating quality in higher education.[25] Seventeen countries — the fifteen member states plus Iceland and Norway — with at least two institutions in each and four in some (making 46 institutions in all) were involved in the study. Two broad discipline areas, engineering sciences and communication, information, art and design were included in the study, one from each institution. At least one university and one non-university institution were involved in each country. In Ireland, the mechanical engineering department in University College Dublin and the graphics department in Limerick Regional Technical College were the participants.

A common methodology was employed for evaluating the teaching and learning in these discipline areas. Each such discipline area carried out and documented a self-assessment, giving details on the institutional context, aims and objectives, programme, students, staff and management of human resources, facilities, quality management, external relationships and strengths and weaknesses. Each discipline area was then subjected to external assessment by a review group of peers. This group prepared an evaluation report that was principally a verification of the self-assessment report, based on a site visit where the group met the authorities of the institution, the self-assessment group, representatives of the student body, staff members and representatives of relevant committees. The peer review group also held an open session, viewed the facilities and visited classrooms to observe teaching. Within each country a national committee, formed specifically for the study, was responsible for appointing the peer review group, organising workshops and other training sessions for the participants, managing the budget and drafting and disseminating a national report.

The methodology used had many of the features of the national systems described above for the United Kingdom, France, Denmark, Netherlands and Sweden.

The general outcome of the study was a resolve to build on the momentum of the project to develop a collaborative network based on the national committees and the national agencies already in existence, to ensure the transfer of experience and the dissemination of developments in methodologies. It was hoped that the results of the study would stimulate national debates on issues of quality evaluation and assurance. There was also some sentiment amongst the participants for a follow up project at European level.

---

[25]European Commission, *Socrates: European Pilot Project for Evaluating Quality in Higher Education, op. cit.*

ORGANISATION FOR ECONOMIC CO-OPERATION AND DEVELOPMENT

There are four programmes within the general framework of the Organisation for Economic Co-operation and Development (OECD) which deal with educational issues. The Centre for Educational Research and Innovation, for instance, regularly produces the publication "Education at a glance; OECD indicators" which provides large databases of comparative indicators about all levels of education in countries throughout the world.[26] The programme on Institutional Management in Higher Education develops policies in the area of quality assurance and higher education management.[27] It is concerned with the impact of quality assurance and assessment systems on the higher education institutions and not on the education itself. In this regard it has pursued a number of projects leading to reports on quality assurance issues such as performance indicators, the interactions between the evaluation process and the decision making process in higher education institutions and quality management, quality assessment and the decision making process.

UNITED NATIONS EDUCATIONAL, SCIENTIFIC AND CULTURAL ORGANISATION

The United Nations Educational, Scientific and Cultural Organisation (UNESCO) has a broad commitment to diversity, relevance and quality in higher education and has devolved its programmes on this topic relating to Europe to its regional European Centre for Higher Education (CEPES), which is based in Bucharest.[28] It published a booklet in 1992 that gives a brief but comprehensive world view of issues of accreditation and quality assurance in higher education.[29] In 1992 it developed a European Group on Academic Assessment (EGAA) as a forum to help to develop a system of assessment and accreditation in higher education in Central and Eastern Europe, but with the issues discussed at the European level. The EGAA is seeking to develop compatible criteria for quality and excellence within the European higher education systems. It collaborates with the different national assessment agencies, collects and disseminates information on academic assessment and accreditation methods, carries out pilot projects and surveys, supports mobility of personnel involved in assessment and accreditation and organises seminars, workshops and conferences on these themes.

---

[26] OECD, *Education at a Glance, op. cit.*
[27] Sterian, P E, *op. cit.*, p. 14.
[28] *Ibid.*, p. 14.
[29] *Ibid.*

EUROPEAN INTER-INSTITUTION ORGANISATIONS

The changing nature of higher education throughout Europe has resulted in over a decade of emphasis on achieving, assuring and improving quality in the service. The need to develop indices of accountability to students, governments, industry and society in general has been a motor force in this process. In the context of increasing international mobility of graduates, an important element of this accountability has been the need for the international recognition of quality standards. This has been reflected in a dramatic ferment amongst the international bodies that represent the higher education institutions.

The Association of European Universities (CRE) has existed since 1959 and has about 520 member institutions in 42 countries.[30] Within CRE each institution is represented by its chief officer (rector, vice-chancellor or president). CRE provides a forum in which the leaders of the European universities meet to discuss mutual problems, co-operate and help universities to develop in the context of rapidly changing societies. It has set the following five priority action areas — university restructuring, university financing, interaction with society, promoting cohesion amongst universities and quality improvement. Steering groups have been established in each of these areas to develop programmes of action.

In relation specifically to quality issues, CRE has focussed on quality audit and review at the level of the institution's mechanisms of quality management, and not on educational and research processes. The emphasis therefore has been on strategic management of quality, to enable the development in the long run of a quality culture and a common understanding of quality assessment. During 1994 and 1995 CRE carried out a pilot project to quality audit the Universities of Gothenburg, Utrecht and Oporto. As a result, in 1996 a second expanded pilot scheme was begun. In this scheme, ten universities in Portugal, Spain, Denmark, Germany, Slovenia, Belgium, Czech Republic, Italy and Hungary took part.

A steering committee responsible for the audit is appointed by CRE. This committee appoints the actual audit panel of three rectors or former rectors of European universities. The institution to be audited may not influence the choice of panel members, other than to refuse to accept a member. The audit panel is generally composed of members from countries other than that in which the institution is located. It is responsible for the audit and the even-tual report.

The institution prepares a self-evaluation according to a common struc-ture. This has three chapters on institutional norms, values and constraints, quality culture and capacity for further development. The specific national

---

[30]van Vught, F A, and D F Westerheijden, *op. cit.*

context, resources and problems, as well as the culture and traditions of the institution, are also covered in the self-evaluation report which is not more than 25 pages. The audit team is also supplied with background documentation on higher education in the particular country.

The audit team makes a two-day preliminary visit to the institution to inform the staff of the institution about the nature and form of the audit and to observe the operation and management processes in action.

The main audit visit follows some time later and lasts three days. This includes meetings with the management of the institution, staff members from the central offices, students, academic staff, administrators from the faculties and research areas and external partners of the institution, such as sponsors of research and education projects, local and national government representatives, employers and others. The meetings with the management of the institution are aimed at developing a common understanding of the issues, including the situation, strategy and problems of the institution.

At the end of the main visit, the audit team presents an oral report to the management of the institution, giving the audit team's judgement on the procedures for quality management in the institution. The final written report follows a common recommended structure and is submitted to the institution, which is responsible for the follow-up actions required.

The Liaison Committee of the Confederation of European Rectors' Conferences is the organisation of the national conferences of university chief officers, rectors, vice-chancellors and presidents from EU countries. Those from outside the EU can affiliate as associates. The principal aim of the Liaison Committee is to keep members informed about EU policies in higher education and research. One of its four permanent working groups deals with quality assessment and it has an *ad hoc* group dealing with academic recognition. It co-operates closely with CRE.

In relation to quality assurance, the Liaison Committee emphasises that the aims of an assessment should be relevant and specific to the institution and clearly defined for all participants well in advance.[31] The system of quality assessment, based mostly on a peer review approach, should be the property of the institution. The working group deals with quality assessment in both research and taught programmes. Furthermore it seeks a systematic method for presenting results of quality assessments to facilitate comparisons.

The members of the European Association of Institutions of Higher Education (Eurashe) are chief officers of non-university higher education institutions in Europe and are dedicated to protecting the interests of this educa-

---

[31] Liaison Committee of Rectors' Conferences, *Quality Assessment in European Higher Education* (Brussels) 1992.

tional sector, promoting co-operation and helping to influence EU policies.[32] Based on the principle that quality assurance systems should be the responsibility of institutions themselves, within each member state, Eurashe has participated in the EU Pilot Project and in similar projects in Slovakia and the Czech Republic.

AUSTRALIA

There are 43 universities and university institutions in Australia that offer primary degree courses of three or four years' duration. Master's degrees are offered after one or two further years' study and doctorates require three to five years' study after a primary degree. These higher education institutions are autonomous, with each making its own decisions on matters such as the allocation of funding, staffing and range of academic courses offered.[33]

Until 1988, the higher education system in Australia relied on external examiners to provide the peer review for quality assurance.[34] In that year the Australian Rectors' Committee decided that the universities should have similar curricula for similar courses, while there might be different programmes of courses in the same broad fields. They also replaced the external examiners with a system of Commissions of Academic Standards.

Each commission carries responsibility for a particular discipline or field of study and has a membership of five to seven experts in the field, an expert from outside the educational system and a specialist in educational principles. Over a period of three years a commission visits all the institutions that offer the relevant course, in order to certify the courses and report on the standards and especially the compatibility of standards across the institutions.

THE UNITED STATES

Higher education in the United States is very decentralised and there are technical/vocational institutions, two-year colleges and four-year colleges or universities.[35] The technical/vocational institutions tend to offer training for particular careers. Two-year colleges offer both terminal associate degree qualifications after two years and the first two years of transferable credit for

---

[32]Eurashe, *Quality Management and Quality Assurance in European Higher Education, Methods and Mechanisms*, 1993.
[33]OECD, *Education at a Glance, op. cit.*, pp. 252–253.
[34]Sterian, P E, *op. cit.*, pp. 31–32.
[35]OECD, *Education at a Glance, op. cit.*, pp. 315–316.

a four-year primary degree that may then be taken in a four-year college or university. One year or more of additional study after a primary degree is required in a university for a master's degree while three to five years of study after achieving a primary degree is normally required for a doctorate.

The mechanism for quality assurance in higher education in the United States is that of accreditation of the institution as a whole, not of programmes or discipline areas.[36] Accreditation is the process of evaluation of the institution by an external body, with a view to approving the institution and its curricula for the awarding of different levels of academic awards. While the process is voluntary and does not involve the government, accreditation does accord the institution a level of public trust and gives students and the general public a level of assurance about the quality of the education provided. It is also an important criterion in the allocation of state and federal funding to institutions.

General institutional accreditation is carried out by one of the six private accreditation agencies, each covering a specific region of the United States. Specific professional accreditation is performed by up to eighty professional bodies.[37] The Committee on Post-Secondary Accreditation co-ordinates the work of the accreditation agencies, periodically reviewing their procedures and standards and providing recognition of their work. The Department of Education of the federal government also gives recognition to these agencies, in that it uses their evaluations in the allocation of federal funds.

Broadly the accreditation process is based on evaluating the quality of the outcome of the education process and its general effectiveness, and has the following stages:

- a self-evaluation by the institution

- a visit to the institution by a group of experts nominated by the accreditation agency

- a decision by this group of experts on the level of accreditation of the institution.

SUMMARY

Across the world there is a broad involvement in, and commonality of approach to, quality assurance and quality audit in higher education institutions. These institutions, together with their governments and many international inter-governmental agencies, are deeply involved in the issue,

---

[36]Sterian, P E, *op. cit.*, pp. 25–26.
[37]Phillips, W M, G D Peterson and K B Aberle, "Quality Assurance for Engineering Education in a Changing World", *Int. J. Engng. Ed.*, 16(2), 97–103, 2000.

more than anything else in order to ensure international comparability of the standards of qualifications. In this international context, it is imperative that the higher education institutions in Ireland, in co-operation with the government, establish robust and world class quality assurance and quality audit procedures. To do so it is not necessary to reinvent the wheel, but rather to learn from wide and long international experience.

CHAPTER FOUR

Regulatory and Policy Background to Quality Assurance in Irish Higher Education

Prior to the 1960s the Irish government did not interfere to any significant extent in the internal affairs of the universities and did not openly raise questions about academic decisions and standards.

The expansion of the higher education system and the increased government expenditure on the system over the past thirty years have led to a sea change in the relationships between the government and the higher education institutions.[1] This chapter highlights this change with a particular focus on the emergence of quality assurance as a significant factor in the changing relationships.

COMMISSION ON HIGHER EDUCATION 1960–1967

In 1960, the government established the Commission on Higher Education "to inquire into and make recommendations in relation to university, professional, technological and higher education generally".[2] The Commission was also directed to give attention to "the general organisation and administration of education at those levels and the nature and extent of the provision to be made for such education".

After extensive and lengthy inquiries in Ireland and abroad, the Commission reported in 1967. In its report, the Commission drew attention to the role of the government as the principal provider of finance to the higher education institutions. It highlighted the lack of an overall planning authority for higher education and concluded that essentially no coherent planning was carried out within the sector. It noted that higher education outside the

---

[1] Clancy, P, "The Evolution of Policy in Third-level Education" in Mulcahy, D G and D O'Sullivan, (eds.) *Irish Education Policy: Process and Substance* (Dublin: Institute of Public Administration) 1989.

[2] Commission on Higher Education 1960–1967, I. *Presentation and Summary of Report*, (Baile Átha Cliath: Oifig an tSoláthair) 1967.

universities had "remained comparatively under-developed". It drew attention to academic weaknesses in the universities at undergraduate level due to "increasing numbers of students, low entry standards and inadequate staffing and accommodation", and at postgraduate research level. The Commission also called for improvements in university governance and academic appointment procedures. Clearly the Commission was preoccupied to a significant extent with issues which might now be categorised as "quality assurance" and their close relationship to planning and management in higher education.

While the Commission emphasised the government's support for the autonomy of the universities, it saw as necessary the limitation of the universities' autonomy, particularly where the institutions received large subventions of public funds. The report clearly expressed the contradiction for the government, in being the authority deciding on the amounts of public funds to be devoted to higher education, and yet, in a situation of institutional autonomy, having only limited control over how such funds were utilised. The Commission proposed that a planning and regulating agency be established to provide a buffer agency between the institutions and the government, somewhat in the manner of the University Grants Commission (UGC) in Britain. The agency would not only plan and administer the state grants to the institutions, but would also be a comprehensive planning authority to preside over the planning and expansion of higher education, then already underway, to serve and match the needs of the country.

HIGHER EDUCATION AUTHORITY ACT 1971

In response to the report of the Commission on Higher Education, the Government set up the Higher Education Authority (HEA) on an *ad hoc* basis in 1968. The Authority was statutorily established under the provisions of the Higher Education Authority Act 1971, which set out its functions. Among these functions, "the development of higher education", the "promotion of the attainment of equality of opportunity in higher education and the democratisation of its structures" might be interpreted, perhaps indirectly, as quality assurance issues. The direct remit of the HEA included the funding of the universities and other designated institutions. In addition it was given advisory powers in relation to the full range of issues arising in higher education.

In this respect neither the HEA Act nor the HEA, as established, addressed a number of the concerns of the Commission on Higher Education in relation to standards and quality. The universities themselves retained almost complete autonomy over the internal distribution of their allocated resources. Since its establishment the role of the HEA has been to facilitate the general autonomy and academic freedom of the institutions under its aegis. Issues concerning the standards of programmes within the institutions were not brought within its remit. Indeed not until the discussions leading to the Universities Act 1997 were quality assurance issues addressed.

NATIONAL COUNCIL FOR EDUCATIONAL AWARDS ACT 1979

The Commission on Higher Education recommended in 1967 the establishment of what it termed "New Colleges" in Limerick and Dublin. It also recommended that a Technological Authority be established to monitor industry requirements as well as qualifications and their standards in technological areas. Soon after the inception of the HEA in 1968, the Minister for Education referred to it the "question of establishing a body which would award national qualifications at technician and technologist levels". The following year, the HEA recommended the establishment of a National Council for Educational Awards (NCEA) which would have the power "to grant certificates, diplomas and degrees to persons who have successfully pursued courses of study at third-level educational institutions other than universities".[3] In response the government established the NCEA on an *ad hoc* basis in 1972.

Seven years later, following the enactment of the National Council for Educational Awards Act 1979, the Council was given statutory powers to provide for national educational awards — degrees, diplomas and certificates — in a range of non-university institutions in Ireland. The institutions concerned included the National College of Art and Design (NCAD), the National Institutes for Higher Education (NIHEs) in Limerick and Dublin, the third-level colleges (now the Dublin Institute of Technology) of the City of Dublin Vocational Education Committee (CDVEC), Thomond College of Education in Limerick, all the Regional Technical Colleges (RTCs, retitled in 1997/1998 as regional Institutes of Technology or ITs) and any other institution specified in an order by the Minister for Education under the Act.

Significantly, the NCEA was given a range of what would now be recognised as quality assurance functions in respect of the designated institutions. According to the Act, the Council was empowered to grant degrees, diplomas, certificates or other educational awards to persons who successfully completed courses approved by the Council and attained a satisfactory standard in approved examinations or in approved programmes of research. The Council could also recognise a degree, diploma, certificate or other educational award granted to persons who successfully completed specific approved courses. It could approve of such courses of study or instruction if it was satisfied that the standard in general corresponded to

---

[3] Higher Education Authority, *A National Council for Educational Awards and a College of Higher Education at Limerick* (Dublin) 1969.

relevant standards in universities. The Council could assess the standard maintained by any institution to which the Act applied in relation to any course of study or instruction approved by the Council.

Thus, the NCEA was empowered to accredit institutions, validate and review programmes of study, ensure that approved courses had equivalent standards to similar courses in the universities, and confer awards — all key elements in any scheme of quality assurance.

From its inception the NCEA developed quality assurance procedures based on the accreditation of institutions, the initial validation and periodic review of courses and the appointment of external examiners in respect of those examinations moderated by the NCEA for its awards.[4]

NATIONAL INSTITUTES OF HIGHER EDUCATION ACTS 1980

The National Institute of Higher Education (NIHE) (Limerick) was established in 1969 as the second part of the response to the 1969 HEA report. The plan was for its graduates to receive NCEA awards and this was what happened until 1974, when the government withdrew degree awarding power from the NCEA. In that year NIHE (Limerick) was accredited for degree awards by the National University of Ireland (NUI). In 1976 it was made a recognised college of the NUI. With the passing of the National Institute of Higher Education (Limerick) Act 1980, the Institute was removed from the NUI and again brought under the aegis of the NCEA, to which degree awarding power had been restored in 1977.

The National Institute of Higher Education (Dublin) was established by the government in 1974 and its first governing body was appointed in 1975. It had emerged from a process begun five years earlier when the CDVEC engaged in a planning exercise with the Minister for Education to provide a Technological/Higher Education College at Ballymun, the so-called "Ballymun Project". In the event NIHE (Dublin) was set up independent of the CDVEC and from its inception came under the aegis of the NCEA.

Two identical Acts, the NIHE (Limerick) Act and the NIHE (Dublin) Act, were passed in 1980 to place the two NIHEs in Limerick and Dublin on a statutory footing. These Acts defined the functions of the NIHEs in relation to academic quality, standards and levels of programmes, as providing primary degree, diploma, certificate as well as postgraduate level courses and engaging in research work. The NIHEs did not have any awarding power but were thereafter accredited by the NCEA and their graduates received NCEA degrees.

---

[4] National Council for Educational Awards, *Examinations Marks and Standards 1998* (Dublin) 1998.

With regard to academic quality assurance, the Academic Council of each NIHE was empowered to offer appropriate programmes of study and to establish appropriate structures to implement them, develop research, put academic regulations in place, conduct examinations, evaluate academic progress of students and organise tutorial and other academic counselling for students.

Issues of standards and the assurance of quality were not explicitly addressed in these Acts. By 1986 the role of the NCEA in relation to quality assurance in the NIHEs involved the approval of courses based on an institutional self-evaluation and the participation of university and business specialists from Ireland and abroad in curriculum development and Boards of Study. It also involved the appointment of external examiners from nominations of academic and business experts submitted by the institutions. Arrangements for the admission of students were devolved to the institutions themselves, subject to government policies and regulations set out by the Central Applications Office (CAO).

INTERNATIONAL STUDY GROUP ON TECHNOLOGICAL EDUCATION 1987

The lobbying by the NIHEs to improve their status persuaded the Minister for Education in 1986 to establish an International Study Group to examine technological education outside the universities and advise on the case for a new technological university.[5] Remarkably, this process was instituted and carried out with little direct involvement by the HEA, which would have seemed the appropriate vehicle for such a study.

Amongst the terms of reference of the group were the following:

- to examine the arrangements for the provision of third level technological education outside the University colleges

- to consider the purpose and functions of the NIHEs in Limerick and Dublin, their present stage of development and the level of technological courses provided in them

- to consider the question of whether, if a Technological University were established, it might include constituent colleges in addition to NIHE (Limerick) and NIHE (Dublin)

- to consider the types and level of degrees, and conditions for their award, to be awarded by the Technological University if established.

---

[5] *Technological Education*, Report of the International Study Group to the Minister for Education, 1987.

The tasks of the group may now be recognised as broadly touching on quality audit or accreditation of higher education in general and of the two NIHEs in particular. This was the first occasion that any such process had been undertaken in the Irish Republic.

Before the International Study Group visited the two NIHEs, each prepared a profile of its management and academic structures, programmes and activities. When the Group visited each institution, it met the directors and members of staff and viewed teaching and research areas.

To complete its work, the Group also met representatives of the universities, the fifteen non-university technological institutions, the NCEA (which at that time accredited the courses and research programmes within the NIHEs) and professional bodies and other representative groups.

The International Study Group considered institutional management and planning, as well as matters relating to academic standards and quality assurance and outlined significant recommendations about them in its report. It recommended that the HEA "should be fully involved in all matters relating to the planning, financing and co-ordination of all third-level activities". In relation to the NIHEs it was the Study Group's view that their standards of scholarship were as high as those of the universities and that they should be given the title and status of self-accrediting universities. It recommended that their legislation should be amended to "give them degree awarding powers and to provide statutory Academic Councils with responsibility" for their academic affairs.

The group recommended that the NIHEs in Limerick and Dublin should be established as universities, the NIHE (Limerick) having the title University of Limerick and the NIHE (Dublin) having the title Dublin City University or University of Leinster.

The report also recommended that the Dublin Institute of Technology and the Regional Technical Colleges be established on a statutory basis with their funding arrangements being made through the HEA. These measures would give these institutions increased autonomy and allow them to engage in research, development and consultancy services for external organisations.

In 1989, two Acts of the Oireachtas were enacted to confer university status on the University of Limerick and Dublin City University.

EDUCATION FOR A CHANGING WORLD — GREEN PAPER 1992

The emergence of academic quality assurance as a distinct concern in higher education in the Republic of Ireland had not occurred by the end of the 1980s, in spite of the fact that, at that stage, quality assurance had been a major theme in British and mainland European higher education for more than a decade. For instance, in a comprehensive review of educational policy issues in Ireland, published in 1989, there was no reference to quality assurance or to matters of academic standards that are now accepted as pertaining to academic quality assurance.[6]

The terminology of quality assurance probably first entered the public education debate in Ireland with the publication by the Minister for Education of the Green Paper on education in 1992.[7] Indeed this document indicated many areas for legitimate questioning in relation to quality in higher education. It referred to "the concern and care for the students and the ways in which this is demonstrated in the institution; the quality of teaching and support provided by staff; the percentage of new entrants who proceed to graduation; the output and quality of research; the efficient use of resources and the procedures in place in institutions to review quality continually". In particular it envisaged quality assurance in higher education to be founded on twin pillars, one internal and one external. The internal foundation would be the development of performance indicators and quality review procedures within the institutions. The external foundation would be the appropriate monitoring and assistance to the institutions through an audit unit within the HEA. It saw as a key measure the improvement of the quality of teaching, guidance and assistance available to students through appropriate staff development.

The Green Paper addressed a number of other aspects of quality assurance. It suggested that the institutions, and in particular the universities, should have maximum flexibility in developing courses, but that, within the constraints of policy, budget and physical resources, courses should be run cost-efficiently and should not adversely affect other courses.

In relation to the DIT and the RTCs, the Green Paper suggested that an appropriate, but unspecified, balance between certificate, diploma and degree graduates be maintained and that the value of certificate and diploma awards as terminal qualifications should not be undermined. It advised that any degree courses developed should not be offered less cost-effectively than by a university, and should be aimed at a proven industrial need based on effective liaison with and support from industry. It suggested that the NCEA would approve the programmes and report annually to the Department of Education on the national and local patterns of course development. The Green Paper also recommended that the NCEA undertake a review of entry standards to courses in the DIT and the RTCs, together with the student success and retention records. This review was envisaged as being linked to a review of standards of achievement in each of the colleges.

While many of these recommendations have not yet been implemented, it is of some significance that a quality assurance role was, at that stage, proposed for the HEA in respect of the universities, and a similar and possibly more

---

[6] Mulcahy, D G and D O'Sullivan (eds), *Irish Educational Policy: Process and Substance, op. cit.*

[7] An Roinn Oideachais, *Education for a Changing World* (Baile Átha Cliath: Oifig an tSoláthair) 1992.

centralised role was being proposed for the NCEA in respect of the DIT and the RTCs.

DUBLIN INSTITUTE OF TECHNOLOGY ACT 1992

Following the recommendations contained in the 1986 Green Paper and the report of the International Study Group on Technological Education of 1987, the Dublin Institute of Technology Act 1992 was enacted to establish the DIT as an autonomous institution, independent of the CDVEC, under which its component colleges had previously operated. Among other things, the Act set out the functions of the Institute as being to provide "vocational and technical education and training for the economic, technological, scientific, commercial, industrial, social and cultural development of the State". It gave the Institute the authority to grant diplomas, certificates and other educational awards (excluding degrees) and to enter into arrangements with the NCEA or any university in the State, for the purpose of having degrees granted. The Act also empowered the Institute to engage in research, consultancy and development work. In 1997, after an audit of the quality assurance procedures in the Institute, the Minister for Education made an order under the Act, assigning to the DIT the function of awarding its own primary and postgraduate degrees and honorary awards.

In relation to matters of academic quality assurance, the Academic Council of the DIT was empowered to offer appropriate programmes of study and establish appropriate structures to implement them. It was also empowered to engage in research and development, select, admit, retain or exclude students, put academic regulations in place, conduct examinations and evaluate academic progress of students. It could appoint external examiners and organise tutorial and other academic counselling for students. The Act introduced a small element of potential quality audit in the idea of inspection of the Institute whereby an inspector appointed by the Minister for Education would report on the efficiency of the programmes and other activities of the Institute. However, the term "quality assurance" did not appear in the Act.

REGIONAL TECHNICAL COLLEGES ACT 1992

The Regional Technical Colleges Act 1992 was almost identical to the DIT Act. The RTC legislation did not confer upon the RTCs (now regional Institutes of Technology) the power to grant their own academic awards. Furthermore the functions given to their individual Academic Councils did not include the appointment of external examiners or "the conferment of honorary awards". The RTCs were required "to enter into arrangements with the NCEA, with any university in the State or with any other authority approved by the

Minister from time to time for the purpose of having degrees, diplomas, certificates or other educational awards" granted.

COMPTROLLER AND AUDITOR GENERAL (AMENDMENT) ACT 1993

Under the Comptroller and Auditor General (Amendment) Act 1993, the Comptroller and Auditor General has the authority to audit the accounts of certain designated organisations, such as third-level educational institutions, which receive funding from the Government. In the course of such an audit she/he is empowered to carry out such audit tests as are considered appropriate to ensure that:

- "the receipts and expenditures recorded in the accounts are supported by substantiating documentation"

- the amounts expended have been applied by the organisation concerned "for the purposes for which the appropriation made by the Oireachtas was intended"

- "the transactions recorded in the accounts conform with the authority under which they purport to have been carried out".

The Comptroller and Auditor General may further inquire into whether the resources of the organisation have been used economically and efficiently, generally in comparison with other similar organisations. In carrying out the basic financial audit and any such further investigations, he/she is entitled to access to any relevant documents and records from the organisation.

A report on this audit and any further examination is prepared by the Comptroller and Auditor General and laid before the houses of the Oireachtas. This report is expected to detail any ways in which the audit is deficient in relation to the criteria outlined above.

GOVERNMENT WHITE PAPER 1995

The government's comprehensive White Paper on education, published in April 1995, set out the background and policy framework against which future developments in Irish education, including higher education, would be progressed.[8] The White Paper identified the following considerations as those

---

[8] An Roinn Oideachais, Government White Paper, *Charting our Education Future* (Baile Átha Cliath: Oifig an tSoláthair) 1995.

that would underpin the approach that would be pursued in relation to higher education:

- the promotion of equality in and through higher education

- the recognition of the legitimate autonomy of institutions, particularly in relation to determining the educational aims and content of programmes

- the promotion of the highest standards of quality

- the preservation of diversity and balance of provision, within the system, while avoiding unnecessary overlap or duplication

- the promotion and facilitation of the key leadership role of higher education as a source of social and economic development, together with the need to ensure continuing relevance to the needs of the economy and the promotion of links between institutions and their social and economic environments

- the continuous development of a framework of accountability for individual institutions and for the higher education system as a whole

- the provision of an appropriate legislative framework, which affirms well-established values while reflecting the role of higher education in modern society.

Interestingly the White Paper discussed quality assurance in higher education under the general heading of accountability, indicating the main origin of government concern in the matter. The White Paper noted how the Report on the National Education Convention in 1994 had stated that the development of good quality assurance procedures was a "central task of management in higher education institutions", to achieve the highest standards of quality for the "benefit of students, society and the economy".[9] It emphasised that quality is the "hallmark that underpins the status and mobility of graduates both nationally and internationally".

While it acknowledged that quality assurance was a complex issue, it highlighted the contradiction between autonomy and accountability, the widespread acceptance in higher education of the need for accountability in relation to public funds and the worry that such accountability and efficiency should not diminish academic control of key academic matters. The checks and balances needed to resolve this contradiction would consist of appropriate and rigorous peer review of individuals and departments in the higher educational institutions.

These institutions would be responsible for putting quality assurance

---

[9] National Education Convention Secretariat, *Report on the National Education Convention* (Dublin) 1994.

procedures in place. Overall, quality auditing systems would also be developed by the institutions under the general aegis of the HEA. These systems would consist of periodic evaluation of departments and faculties by national and international peers, in each case following individual internal self-study by the department or faculty itself. The implementation of the recommendations of such audits would be monitored and appropriate performance indicators developed to allow comparison with national and international benchmarks. In order to help weak departments, faculties and institutions and to minimise the possible penal aspect of such evaluations, the White Paper proposed that a comprehensive national programme of staff development for higher education teachers be established.

STEERING COMMITTEE ON THE FUTURE DEVELOPMENT OF HIGHER EDUCATION 1995

In its 1995 Report, the Steering Committee on the Future Development of Higher Education made proposals and recommendations on a number of issues — the future growth of higher education in Ireland, the distribution of the growth as between university and non-university institutions and geographically, the financial implications of the growth and the involvement of non-standard students (disadvantaged, mature and second-chance) in higher education.[10]

Quality assurance in the system was a key consideration in forming its recommendations. It noted that in spite of the expansion of the system up to 1992, the quality of the students entering with Leaving Certificate continued to improve and the "quality and international acceptability of the graduate output" had been maintained. The capacity of the system was strained, however, and it was concerned that further expansion should not occur at the expense of quality. An effective system of quality assurance would be needed "to ensure public accountability and transparency and ... continuing confirmation and validation of academic standards". This system would involve "self-evaluation supported by peer review and quality audit". It envisaged that the requisite internal institutional process would be overseen by the HEA, under an enlarged remit, so as to minimise "the bureaucratic requirements of reporting while ensuring effective accountability and transparency".

---

[10]Higher Education Authority, *Report of the Steering Committee on the Future Development of Higher Education (Based on a Study of Needs to the Year 2015)* (Dublin) 1995.

UNIVERSITIES ACT 1997

The Universities Act of 1997 had a number of aims and aspects relating to drawing all the universities in the Republic of Ireland into broadly standard structures and internal regulatory frameworks. It was the first piece of academic legislation to specifically set out *inter alia* the responsibilities of the institutions for academic quality assurance. The Act also set out terms and conditions for the autonomy of the institutions.

Among the functions elaborated under this legislation for underpinning the autonomy of a university were the maintenance, management and administration of the property, money, assets and rights of the university, acquisition and disposal of land or other property and acceptance of gifts of money, land or other property. The university has "the right and responsibility to preserve and promote the traditional principles of academic freedom in the conduct of its internal and external affairs". It is entitled to regulate its affairs in accordance with its independent ethos and traditions and the traditional principles of academic freedom, but under the limitations of being duty-bound to promote and preserve equality of opportunity and access, using resources effectively and efficiently and being publicly accountable. At the level of the individual member of academic staff, they are free, "within the law, in her/his teaching, research and any other activities in or outside the university, to question and test received wisdom, to put forward new ideas and to state controversial or unpopular opinions and should not be disadvantaged, or subject to less favourable treatment by the university, for the exercise of that freedom".

In relation to academic quality assurance, one of the objects of a university is specified as promoting "the highest standards in, and quality of, teaching and research". The Act empowers the university, in relation to staff recruitment, to develop transparent interview and other procedures to ensure participation of high quality candidates in the recruitment process, and thereby attract high quality academic staff. The Act also extends the ideas of quality in a social direction, requiring the university to "have regard to the attainment of gender balance and equality of opportunity among the students and employees of the university" and "promote access to the university and to university education by economically or socially disadvantaged people and by people from sections of society significantly under-represented in the student body".

Each university is to have an academic council which would have the responsibility to design and develop programmes of study, establish structures to implement those, develop research, manage the selection, admission, retention and exclusion of students, develop statutes to regulate the academic affairs of the university, including the conduct of examinations, the determination of examination results, the procedures for appeals by students relating to the results of such examinations and the evaluation of academic progress, recommend the awarding of fellowships, scholarships, bursaries, prizes or other awards and arrange tutorial or other academic counselling for students.

In a new departure for universities in Ireland, the legislation requires each university to prepare a strategic development plan, setting out the aims of the university for its operation and development, including its strategy for achieving these aims, and for carrying out the functions of the university, during a period of three years or more. This allows each university to be examined in respect of its strategic plan and, indeed, audited in relation to its achievement of the plan.

The Universities Act specifically requires each university to "establish procedures for quality assurance aimed at improving the quality of education and related services provided by the university". These procedures are to include the evaluation, at regular intervals not less than once every ten years, of each department and faculty of the university and any service provided by the university, by employees of the university in the first instance (a self-study) and assessment by those, including students, availing of the teaching, research and other services provided by the university (part of the self-study), as well as evaluation by persons, other than employees, who would be competent to make national and international comparisons on the quality of teaching and research and the provision of other services at university level (an element of external audit). The findings of such evaluation and assessment are to be published by the governing authority of the university. The university is required to implement any findings arising out of such an evaluation, unless, having regard to the resources available to the university or for other reasons, it would be impractical or unreasonable to do so. Furthermore the university has to periodically (at least every fifteen years) review and publish the effectiveness of these internal evaluation and external assessment procedures as well as the implementation of the findings arising from these procedures.

The university legislation introduced another possible element of external audit in the university visitor, who could be asked by the Minister for Education to inquire into the academic or other affairs of the university, if there were reasonable grounds for considering that the functions of the university were being performed in a manner that might be in breach of the regulations of the university.

The Universities Act effected a number of significant changes in the role of the HEA in relation to the higher education institutions designated under its remit, particularly in relation to academic quality assurance matters. For instance the HEA is now required to review the strategic development plan of each institution, monitor the implementation of the plan and publish a report on such review and monitoring. The HEA is also to review and report on the procedures established by each university for evaluating the quality of its teaching and research. Significantly, under this legislation, the HEA is entrusted with monitoring and publishing reports on the implementation of the institution's policies on equality and access. The HEA has a further role in setting the staffing levels and relative priorities between different activities in a university, in that it may issue guidelines on the numbers and grades of employees in the university and also the part of the budget to be applied to the different activities of the university. Finally the HEA may place restrictions and conditions on the use of moneys it pays to a university.

QUALIFICATIONS (EDUCATION AND TRAINING) ACT 1999

As proposed in the government's White Paper on education, the Minister for Education established Teastas, to become a national certification authority in September 1995 on a preparatory, interim basis.[11]

To implement the 1997 proposals of Teastas, the Qualifications (Education and Training) Act 1999 proposed the establishment of a National Qualifications Authority (NQA). The objectives of this Authority will be to establish and maintain a framework for the "development, recognition and award of qualifications in the State ... based on standards of knowledge, skill or competence to be acquired by learners". The NQA will also establish, promote and maintain the standards of awards of the new Further Education and Training Awards Council, the new Higher Education and Training Awards Council, the Dublin Institute of Technology and any university established under section nine of the 1997 Universities Act. Furthermore it will "promote and facilitate access, transfer and progression" within this framework.

Quality assurance and related issues fundamentally underpin this Act which posited a national framework. However, the existing universities will not come under the aegis of the NQA, leaving a major discontinuity in the national character of the framework of qualifications and procedures. The NQA will, at most, "facilitate and advise" universities in relation to procedures for "access, transfer and progression" of students.

There will be a valuable international dimension to the framework in that the NQA will liaise with educational and other bodies abroad to facilitate the mutual recognition of awards.

The Authority will also be required to be informed of the training and education needs of industry in the broadest sense, nationally and internationally and of the relevant education and training practices in other countries.

The two new Councils, the Further Education and Training Awards Council and the Higher Education and Training Awards Council, are also to be established by this legislation, each as an awarding body. Each of the Councils will determine the policies and criteria for the making of its particular awards and will separately validate and monitor the quality of programmes leading

---

[11] *Charting our Education Future, op. cit.*, pp. 82–83; Teastas, *First Report* (Dublin) 1997.

to these awards. The Act outlined the broad procedures for the validation of such a programme.

The institution that will provide such a programme will establish its own quality assurance and enhancement procedures. These procedures will include "evaluation at regular intervals" by "persons who are competent to make national and international comparisons", "evaluation by learners of that programme", evaluation of related services and publication of "findings arising out of the application of those procedures". Furthermore the Authority may make recommendations to the providing institution arising from these procedures. It will also be entitled to review the effectiveness of the procedures and the implementation of recommendations arising from them.

Broadly similar quality assurance procedures will be required by the Authority of the Dublin Institute of Technology and any new university established under the section nine process of the Universities Act 1997, even though in each of these cases the institution would have its own academic awarding authority. Under the Act of 1999, the DIT and any future section nine universities are required to review the effectiveness of their quality assurance procedures not more than once every three years but not less than once every seven years. This is in contrast to the absurdly long fifteen-year review cycle required of the universities designated under the Universities Act of 1997.

The Act also required some amendments to the Universities Act, outlined previously, and to the HEA Act of 1971. In relation to quality assurance matters provided for in the Universities Act, the HEA is to consult with the NQA in advising the universities. Any section nine university (but not any existing university) will submit its strategic plan to the Authority for approval, a provision not envisaged in the Universities Act. Also a section nine university established under the Universities Act will not be governed by the quality assurance sections of the Universities Act but rather by the procedures of this Act.

Postgraduate research activities and the quality assurance processes required in such work received no overt attention in this Act.

SUMMARY

After almost a decade of study, discussion and government policy statements, there is now in place a legislative framework for quality assurance in higher education. The very fact that this framework is sketchy and not strongly prescriptive allows the institutions to develop their procedures from their own histories and to organically implant them as routine elements of their day-to-day work. The stage is set, therefore, for the application and development of quality assurance and quality audit procedures in all the higher education institutions in Ireland over the next few years.

CHAPTER FIVE

Guidelines for the Design and Validation of a New Course

Procedures for the quality assurance of an individual course begin with its initial design and validation.[1]

COURSE CONCEPTION

A proposal for a new course should normally be submitted sufficiently in advance of the proposed starting date to allow time for its development and validation and for the necessary marketing processes to advise potential students appropriately.

It is an important aspect of the role and function of the academic leadership within an institution to be actively informed about relevant local, national and international developments, which may suggest directions for new course development and the contrary process of phasing out courses currently running.

One or more staff members from a department or departments in the institution may initiate a new course proposal. The inspiration for such a proposal may arise from the experience and observations of those staff members in their discipline, or from the ways in which the discipline may be changing and how the relevant professional body may be developing. The idea for a course may also arise from their research activities or from their consultancy experiences with businesses, industries and/or public bodies. Industrial developments, technology foresight activities and government reports, regulatory initiatives by national and local government agencies, as well as planned expansion of industrial sectors, can also provide the inspiration for a new course.

The preliminary course planning process is a vital element in setting solid foundations for a new course. It is important that a series of phases be put in place in this process, involving elements of feedback and confidence

---

[1] Dublin Institute of Technology, *Course Quality Assurance Handbook* (Dublin) 2nd edition, 1997.

building for the proposing team and sharpening the focus and direction of the course.

In order to facilitate the course development process, it is essential that a preliminary course proposal be formulated for discussion and consideration. Such a proposal requires details on the following fundamental aspects of the course:

- title and academic award sought

- support for the course from industry, commerce, government agencies, etc.

- associated professional bodies and their involvement or support

- market demand, both by industry for graduates with the range of knowledge and skills to be acquired on the course and by potential students

- relevance of the new course to the mission and strategic plan of the institution as a whole and of the departments and faculties concerned, its impact on courses and programmes currently on offer and on the human and physical resources available

- philosophy and aims

- objectives and value to be added to students by the course

- mode of delivery (full time, part time, modularised, other) and duration

- modes of teaching, learning and examination envisaged

- numbers of students planned over an initial five year period

- academic entry requirements for year one

- advanced student transfer arrangements from other courses or institutions into later years of the course, including recognition of prior experiential learning

- industrial or other links, including possible work placement

- main subjects, their relative contributions in each year and the integration of the course elements

- curriculum hours in each year (lectures, practical or studio, tutorial, others)

- student workload in each year

- accommodation available and required in each year

- equipment and resources available and required in each year

- academic staff available and additional staff required in each year

- full time staff recruitment required and time scale for their recruitment

- technical support staff available and additional staff required

- administrative staff available and additional staff required

- staff development required to run and develop the course

- possible future development of the course.

The formulation of the preliminary course proposal obviously requires substantial work by the staff members proposing the course. The process of formulating this proposal is also an iterative one involving discussion with and feedback from colleagues, local department and faculty managers, as well as from industry, government agencies, professional bodies and society in general. The preliminary course proposal should constitute a persuasive case to the authorities of the institution and, if necessary, to the Department of Education and Science, for the allocation of the necessary resources — personnel, accommodation, equipment — to deliver the course over the planned time scale.

At each academic and administrative level in the institution, the preliminary course proposal should be assessed in terms of both its academic aspects and the resources required to deliver it. These aspects must be viewed in the context of policy priorities, available resources and resources to be acquired. Thus the local faculty authorities must consider the feasibility of the proposal, including the impact on its other programmes and activities and how it might alter the balance of provision and the priorities of the faculties and departments involved. If the proposed course requires additional new resources, then the preliminary course proposal and any recommendations of the faculty authorities in this respect must be considered by the executive authorities of the institution. The primary role of the executive authorities at this stage is to ensure that the proposal is consistent with the policy and development plan of the institution, and that adequate resources can be made available to deliver it. The executive advises the faculty authorities of its decision on the proposal and of any conditions attaching to its approval.

When the course proposal has been approved by the executive, the faculty authorities may grant outline planning permission for the course, thereby allowing the proposing team to proceed to design and develop the detailed course documentation required for the validation process of the institution. Outline planning permission for the course does not guarantee that the proposed course will receive validation or, if it were validated, that the course would be offered in any particular year.

The faculty authorities then approve the establishment of a course planning team — generally expanded from the original proposing team — under a nominated chairperson, to draft the course documentation for the validation process. In drafting the course documentation, the planning course team draws upon expertise within the departments and faculties involved, and indeed, the institution as a whole, and should call on external expertise where considered appropriate.

For ease of processing and evaluation, it is desirable that the institution should use a common template for the documentation it requires for the validation process. Although this documentation could be prepared in many different formats, it should include two broad categories of documentation:

1. background information to explain, underpin, support and justify the establishment of the new course, and

2. the course document to describe the structure, curriculum and regulations for the new course. The course document, when approved, is made available through the library to all students on the course to help guide them in their approach to successfully undertaking the course.

The background information would contain detailed accounts of the following:

- *market demand and support* — documentary evidence on the need for the course, of the market, and of support from other departments, faculties and external organisation(s)

- *accommodation/resources available to run course* — how the course is to be accommodated, specialised equipment and facilities available in departments involved, laboratory and lecture room accommodation, relevant library stock, computer facilities, media resources, additional facilities and equipment required to operate the new course

- *staff* — listing of staff to teach on the course, with their qualifications and the subjects to be taught by each, time allocations, etc., detailed CVs for all such staff should be supplied, including information on the rest of their duties; research, development and general scholarship activities within the departments involved (especially those which underpin the course and help to support its future development), staff professional development activities and plans

- *course management and quality assurance arrangements* — course management arrangements, membership and chairperson of the course committee, individual year co-ordinators, tutoring arrangements, quality assurance and monitoring procedures, examinations and assessments

- *course development plan* — detailed plans for the development of the course, giving time-scale, etc., teaching and learning enhancement, staff development, enhancement of facilities

- any other documentation that the course planning team considers appropriate.

The course document should comprise the following:

- *course background and structure* — introduction to the faculty, department, staff specialities, other courses currently offered, facilities available to run the course, etc., title of course, award sought and date of submission, course aims and objectives, nature, duration and general structure of course, relationships with professional and academic bodies, department and course advisory boards, etc.

- *admission criteria* —admission requirements and procedures, procedures for non-standard applicants, advanced stage transfer procedures, etc.

- *curriculum, examinations and syllabuses* — course curriculum, class timetables, giving contact hours, teaching methods (lecture, seminar, tutorials, workshops, practicals, others) and course credits, estimated student workload, schedule of examinations, structure and weighting of each examination, marks and standards, regulations for progress to next stage, compulsory and optional course elements, compensation arrangements, diagrams showing alternative pathways through the course, details of each subject/component course including aims (what teacher wishes to achieve), objectives (what students should be able to do), general subject matter (including rationale and relevance to overall course and integration with other component courses), syllabus (detailed listing of contents of subject matter, with estimate of the learning hours required for each main section), strategy for delivery (teaching approach and methods), examination methods (including weightings), credits allocated (European Credit Transfer System or ECTS) and essential and background reading lists.

This documentation is submitted for comment and endorsement to the head of department, the heads of collaborating departments and also to the head of any external collaborating organisation, where appropriate. They are then forwarded to the faculty authorities for consideration.

The faculty authorities review the course documentation to assess whether it is appropriate for submission to a validation panel and meets the requirements of an external body where this might be involved. The faculty authorities may set up a sub-group within the faculty to interact with the course planning team to discuss the documentation. When the course documentation is approved at this level, it is forwarded for validation.

VALIDATION

Validation is the institution's formal process of requiring a validation panel to assess a proposed new course for an academic award, to ensure that it meets the requirements and standards for that award. The favourable outcome of the validation process is the approval of the new course for delivery. In order to inform its judgement, the validation panel visits the faculty to consider the course documentation, discuss the proposed course with the planning team and students and graduates of the faculty and view the facilities available for the course.

The academic council, in consultation with the faculty authorities, is responsible for constituting the validation panel. In order to comprise the objective expertise required, the validation panel should include internal and external peers familiar with current practice and developments in the relevant disciplines, but who are largely independent of the department(s) proposing the course and some of whom are independent of the institution. It is also desirable that members be chosen who are experienced in industry, commerce, the public sector or the relevant profession. They should possess an understanding of teaching, learning and examination work in higher education, be familiar with the institution or with similar institutions and have an awareness of the general requirements for academic awards at the level proposed for the new course. The validation panel should not be too large because of the difficulty in assembling a large group of people with heavy commitments for the number of days required for a validation event.

Typically, the validation panel consists of:

- at least three persons from inside the institution including a chairperson, generally a senior academic from a faculty not involved in offering the course, a member with particular responsibility for quality assurance and at least one member of staff not involved with the course, from the faculty proposing the course but from a department other than the proposing department

- at least two external members, nominated by the faculty authority, at least one a senior academic in the discipline and at least one a senior professional or industrial practitioner in a related discipline.

In general, external panel members should have no recent connection with the institution. Any such previous connection should be declared at an early stage to ensure the maximum objectivity in the work of the validation panel.

Internal and/or external observers as considered appropriate may be recommended by the faculty authorities to work with the validation panel. A senior academic member of staff, independent of the faculty involved should be nominated to act as secretary and organiser of the validation panel.

The validation panel is required to make an impartial peer judgement on the standard, content and conduct of the proposed course and on its comparability with other courses elsewhere in the country and/or internationally. It decides whether or not the graduates of the course should be eligible to be conferred with the proposed award.

The general issues considered and evaluated by the validation panel encompass the following:

- *course background and structure* — principles and philosophy underpinning the course (market, national and local relevance and demand), features, rationale for the development of the course, relationship of the course to the other courses and programmes in the department and faculty and to the faculty/department plans and the institutional plans, aims and objectives, expected intellectual development and learning experience of a student taking the course

- *physical resources* — facilities available to the course and, in the context of their being shared with other courses and programmes, their adequacy to ensure the standard proposed, lecture rooms, laboratories, library, journals, IT access, and other infrastructural support

- *staff* — staff profile, quality and level of staffing available to the course, availability in the light of other commitments, research, scholarly and professional work, publications and staff development activities which underpin the standard of the course and help to ensure the maintenance of standards, recruitment and staff renewal policies and practices, liaison with other departments and faculties and with other third level institutions in Ireland and abroad, liaison with industry, commerce, public agencies, professional bodies and relevant international academic and other agencies

- *admission criteria* — clarity of the student admission criteria at all stages, and of the criteria for student progression from one stage of the course to the next; projected student numbers, mature students

- *curriculum, examinations and syllabuses* — relevance and appropriateness of the course content to the aims and objectives set, coherence, how realisable are the standards of the syllabuses, student workload, how well does the examination system proposed measure the extent to which students are likely to achieve the course objectives, appropriateness and progression of the syllabuses throughout the course, integration of the different elements of the course, appropriateness of the academic standard in the final stage of the course to the proposed award

- *course management and quality assurance* — mechanisms for managing the course through the course committee and year co-ordinators and tutors, student support, tutoring and counselling arrangements, student handbook for the course, protection of students' rights, aspects of course which foster study skills, independent learning, individual responsibility and professional behaviour in students, international links and EU dimensions in the course, mechanisms for monitoring the course to maintain the standard of teaching, learning and student performance including student feedback questionnaires and staff feedback schemes, mechanisms for innovation and improvement of the curriculum and reviewing the course at regular intervals, long-term course development plan and how it is proposed to put it into action.

The validation event includes a visit by the validation panel to the department and faculty proposing the new course.

When the validation panel is appointed, each member should be supplied with background information on the institution itself, general guidelines on the role and function of the validation panel, the course documentation prepared by the course planning team, the proposed timetable of the validation event and any other relevant documentation. The documentation should generally be circularised in adequate time for the panel members to study it and to engage in any necessary preliminary consultations.

In preparation for the validation event, the chairperson of the course planning team ensures that copies of the course documentation and all briefing documents are distributed to the members of the course planning team and other staff members involved with the course. The chairperson also organises meetings of the course planning team and other teaching staff who may be associated with the course, to discuss the documentation and prepare to present the course and the course document to the validation panel.

A validation event should have the following features, appropriately scheduled as determined by the panel:

- private meetings of the panel

- introduction of the panel to the senior staff of the faculties and departments involved with the course, the chairperson of the course planning team and other staff, as appropriate

- visit of the panel to facilities available for the course

- meetings with course planning team to discuss specific matters raised by the panel

- meeting with group of current students from comparable courses in the departments and faculties involved

- meeting with group of graduates from the departments and faculties involved

- meeting with staff members teaching on the course to discuss syllabuses, teaching methods, examinations and such related issues.

The validation panel may divide into sub-groups in order to facilitate its work. The discussions at the meetings of the validation panel should be strictly confidential.

The validation panel broadly seeks assurances on a number of key questions — is there a clear need and demand for the course; are the aims and objectives of the course well-founded, clearly formulated and agreed by the course team; do the physical and human resources available and the curricula and teaching schemes proposed, give realistic and achievable substance to these aims and objectives; do the examinations adequately assess the students' learning on the course and, finally, will the graduates of the course possess knowledge, skills and competencies appropriate to the award?

The panel chairperson seeks to clarify the aims of the validation event to the members of the panel, guide the discussion along the lines outlined above, and summarise the conclusions reached by the panel. The validation event should be conducted in a positive, constructive and helpful manner leading to an objective outcome.

At the end of the validation event, the chairperson may make an oral presentation of the findings and conclusions to the senior staff of the department and faculty. The validation panel prepares a written report that may indicate approval or rejection of the proposed course. It may make recommendations for modifying the course and may lay down special conditions for approval.

The details contained in the report should provide comments and recommendations, as considered appropriate, on each of the following aspects of the validation process itself and on the proposed course:

- course documentation provided

- briefing documentation provided

- programme of the visit to the department and faculty

- resources and facilities and how they are shared with other programmes

- staff

- medium term development plan for the course

- findings with regard to the course and the award proposed

- special conditions attached to the findings

- other aspects of the course needing attention

- any other relevant matters.

Each member of the validation panel endorses the report before it is forwarded to the faculty authorities.

A copy of the report is circulated to the chairperson of the course planning team and a formal response is sought from the team. This response is agreed by the head of department and forwarded with observations, where appropriate, to the faculty authorities. The report of the validation panel and the response of the course planning team are formally considered by the faculty authorities and their observations are forwarded to the academic council.

Where the report from the validation panel sets conditions or makes recommendations requiring the proposed course to be modified, the planning course team needs to reconvene and carry out the necessary additional work. The revised course document is then returned for approval to the faculty authorities. These authorities have the responsibility for ensuring and confirming that the conditions and recommendations laid down by the validation panel have been satisfactorily addressed in the revised course document. The revised course document may be subsequently circulated for approval to all members of the validation panel, with confirmation that the stipulated conditions have been met.

When the course has received the final endorsement of the validation panel, and subsequently of the academic council, the faculty authorities ensure that requisite details about the new course are included in the relevant prospectuses, public advertisements and other publications for the information of prospective students.

ACCREDITATION OF A COURSE

Accreditation of a course is a process similar to validation, except that the authority giving approval to the course is an external organisation, professional body or academic institution. Normally the procedure for accreditation is determined by the external organisation and involves carrying out many or all of the stages of validation, described above, in co-operation with that organisation.

APPROVED COURSE DOCUMENT

The approved course document consists of a course document, corrected and modified, as necessary, to include the agreed recommendations and conditions stipulated by the validation panel.

A copy of the approved course document is made available to the faculty head, and a copy is placed in the faculty library, some weeks before the course is scheduled to begin.

STUDENT HANDBOOK FOR THE COURSE

The student handbook is prepared by the course committee for distribution among the students of the course. It should be as brief and clear as possible but should contain the following items:

1. Welcome
    (a) welcome by chairperson of the course committee
    (b) introduction to the institution and a brief outline of its facilities
2. Course details

(a) duration of the course and minimum and maximum periods of registration

(b) list of lecturers teaching on the course with brief details about their work and specialisms

(c) class timetables

(d) list of recommended textbooks and reference materials

(e) estimate of the overall student workload

(f) general schedule of examinations, relative weightings of subjects, arrangements for rechecks and appeals, as well as supplemental examinations

(g) regulations for progression through the course and a clear outline of the pathway(s) through the course

(h) recognition of the course by professional bodies

3. Course management

(a) course committee, year co-ordinators and tutors, staff and student meetings, faculty authorities, examination boards, internal and external examiners, annual monitoring, review

(b) student feedback, staff and student meetings, student representatives on course committee, comments/suggestions box, student survey questionnaire, staff survey questionnaire

(c) course quality assurance procedures

(d) report on quality assurance procedures, including validations, annual course reports and reviews

4. General guidance to the student

(a) attendance requirements

(b) calendar of academic year

(c) planning study programme and study techniques

(d) information on laboratory safety, production of reports

(e) regulations for usage of computer facilities, library, other facilities

(f) general institution regulations on discipline, etc.

(g) other relevant information, such as teaching locations, etc.

(h) relevant student clubs

SUMMARY

The quality assurance procedures used in the design and validation of a new course or programme set a firm foundation and orientation for the course. They help to define the professional and academic ethos of the course and course team, as well as that of the department and institution as a whole.

CHAPTER SIX

Guidelines for the Assurance of Quality in the Operation of an Individual Course

After a course has been duly validated the procedures to assure quality must cover all phases of the operation of the course, including the environment and general context in which it is delivered.[1]

QUALITY ASSURANCE IN COURSE DELIVERY AND MANAGEMENT

Generally the course planning team serves as the core of the course committee for the first academic year, at least, of the operation of the course. During that year the course committee should co-opt student representative(s) into membership. Towards the end of that year the course team can assemble and select a number of additional members as appropriate for the course committee.

As a general guideline a teacher involved on a course should possess a qualification of a level at least equivalent to the level of the terminal award of the course. The subjects taught by a teacher should generally correspond to or be reasonably closely related to the core discipline(s) of their qualification(s).

Staff recruitment and the assignment of teaching tasks in higher education institutions should be guided by these principles.

New members of staff should be inducted carefully into the courses and other programmes in a department. They should be systematically introduced to the philosophy, teaching methodology, teaching aids, handbooks and other documentation, course committees and overall structure and approach of the system. One suitable way of doing this is to appoint a senior member of the department to act as mentor to the new member for the first year or so. Regular workshops, shared between departments and faculties, can also be useful. A

---

[1] Dublin Institute of Technology, *Course Quality Assurance Handbook* (Dublin) 2nd edition 1997.

published code of teaching practice in the institution is an invaluable tool in achieving unity of purpose among the teaching staff.

Because of the changing needs of industry and society and the consequently changing demands on higher education institutions, the need for staff development is also key to ensuring that staff members continue to teach at an appropriate and improving standard throughout their careers. Therefore the institution must have a comprehensive staff development programme that involves all staff members in improving their knowledge and expertise in their discipline, in developing their teaching and administration skills and, in general, in raising their levels of commitment to the institution and to service to their students.

The course committee, in collaboration with the heads of department involved, is responsible for the operation of the course and for reporting on the course to the faculty authorities. It prepares the student handbook for the course, organises staff/student meetings and deals with student, staff and other feedback on the course and its operation. It processes nominations for internal and external examiners and monitors the range of assessments and examinations administered.

It prepares the annual monitoring report on the course. This report incorporates progress on implementing recommendations from previous annual reports, modifications to the course in the light of experience and new developments, staff, student, employer and other feedback and a thorough review of the strengths and weaknesses found in the course during the academic year. In the annual report the course committee comments in particular on the incorporation of the suggestions of the external examiners, the outcome of the student examinations, retention and success rates, the need for staff development and other additional supports needed for the course.

The course committee is also responsible for critically reviewing the course every five years or so, and for preparing the documentation for the review panel, as outlined later in this chapter.

Student feedback on different aspects of a course may be obtained in a number of ways. The presence of student representatives from each year of a course on the course committee can facilitate the students' views being brought to the attention of the course team at the earliest moment. Meetings between senior members of the course committee and student representatives, student membership of departmental academic committees, general staff/student meetings and the use of student comments or suggestion boxes, all can be valuable ways of obtaining student feedback.

Another valuable and relatively open method for student feedback is the questionnaire, which can poll the views of the full student population on a course and allow those views to be graded and quantified. Such a questionnaire, which should be treated confidentially by the course committee, should obtain graded feedback (very good, good, fair, poor) on issues such as the following in respect of each individual course component of the course (lecture courses, tutorials, laboratory or studio work, field trips, work placement, project, etc.):

- overall structure of the course component
- preparedness of student for the course component
- quality of the syllabus content and its relevance
- the balance between theory and practical work
- the relative time allocation to different course elements
- appropriateness of assessment/examination methods
- integration of the different course components into the overall course
- clarity and timeliness of information about the course
- the study and work time required on the course component each week
- lecture and tutorial rooms
- library facilities
- IT facilities and their accessibility
- laboratories and studios
- quality of equipment available
- range of equipment available
- visual aids
- classroom handouts
- learning environment and ethos
- standard of course delivery
- punctuality of teachers
- quality of tutorials
- value of practical work
- project management or supervision
- method(s) of teaching
- interactions with teachers, questions and discussion
- responsiveness to student and other feedback.

Each individual teacher should administer a standard student survey questionnaire on each of their portions of the course. This allows the teacher to analyse the responses and comments and adjust their teaching and presentation to correct perceived weaknesses. It also allows the teacher to supply the course committee with a concise report on the responses and views of the students on their course, including any plans to improve.

The course committee should also administer a standard general student survey on the course as a whole, particularly to obtain the students' views on many of the issues above which are relevant to the course as a whole and its success in achieving an integrated outcome.

Quantitative feedback should also be obtained by the course committee from the staff engaged in teaching on the course. A staff survey question-naire is a simple method of obtaining this feedback which, as well as the matters listed above, should also obtain staff views on such matters as the following:

* preparedness of students for the course

* student responsiveness and participation in the course

* student involvement in paid work outside the institution

* attendance

* integration of component parts of the course

* the administration of the course by the course committee

* quality of communications with other teachers

* responsiveness of the course committee to suggestions

* quality of leadership provided by department and faculty managers

* provision of staff development

* provision of resources/facilities to deliver the course.

A key aspect of all procedures to obtain feedback on courses and programmes is the need for the individual staff members, the course committee and departmental and institutional management, as appropriate, to respond as well and as early as possible to it. The purpose of the feedback is to help to improve the course, to strengthen any weak links and maintain its strong points. If measures are not taken to repair deficiencies pointed out by students and/or staff, within the resources available, this can lead to low student and staff morale and may damage the quality of the course.

Examinations of various kinds — written and practical examinations, practical and project examinations, oral and aural examinations, continuous assessments, examination of supervised professional practice and work placement, examination of written reports and dissertations — are the methods which lecturers and examiners use to measure the performance of students in achieving the objectives of a course. Therefore they constitute a core element in the academic quality assurance procedures of an institution.[2]

All examinations must be administered under formal written regulations and procedures that are clear, widely published and transparently implemented. There may be general cross-institution regulations, as well as course-specific regulations laid down in the approved course document.

In accepting a nomination as an examiner, internal or external, a staff member or outside expert must declare any relevant business, professional or personal interests in respect of any candidates involved in the examinations concerned.

Internal examiners are normally full time or part time members of academic lecturing staff. They are nominated by the relevant head(s) of department and formally appointed each year by the institution. It is essential that the detailed duties and responsibilities of an internal examiner are set out in the regulations of the institution and made available to all examiners. Each such examiner must be familiar with the general and specific regulations in respect of the course(s) for which they are responsible. Broadly, internal examiners prepare and assess such examination materials as are required by the institution and specified in the course document, for the proper conduct of course(s) assigned to them.

In relation to written examinations, internal examiners carry the following responsibilities:

- submission of all draft examination papers in accordance with the dates and conditions specified by the institution

- provision of marking schemes and outline answers or model solutions for each question on each examination paper

- provision of clear instructions to students on each examination paper, specifying the number of questions to be attempted and the marks allocated for each question and part thereof

- clear specification of where special materials or equipment are required or permitted at an invigilated examination and notification of these to the students in advance

- ensuring the maintenance of the established standards for the course and conformity with examination specifications as set out in the regulations and the course document

- employing consistency of terminology and clarity of expression in examination papers while maintaining the relevant standards and conventions of the discipline

---

[2] Dublin Institute of Technology, *General Assessment Regulations* (Dublin) 1st edition, 1998.

- ensuring that the content and overall balance of the examination paper are satisfactory, having regard to the syllabus and the standard of the course and the examination

- where there is more than one internal examiner involved in the preparation of an examination paper, undertaking appropriate consultations concerning the formulation of the examination paper

- giving due consideration to suggestions, criticisms and amendments proposed by the external examiner(s)

- ensuring that proof copies of examination papers are checked for accuracy

- being available for consultation with the examinations office during the entire duration of the examination

- collecting and signing for examination scripts from the examinations office and ensuring that the correct scripts in the correct quantity have been obtained

- when marking candidates' scripts, ensuring that marks awarded are in accordance with the marking scheme submitted and approved for the examination

- marking scripts clearly, indicating the marks awarded to each examination question or part thereof attempted by the candidate

- in accordance with dates determined by the institution, returning all scripts and other assessed materials together with the marks sheet which should clearly show the marks assigned to the various examination questions and the total mark expressed as a percentage

- attending the examination board meeting for the course and participating in determining the overall examination result for each candidate

- maintaining the strict confidentiality of the proceedings and deliberations of examination board meetings.

In relation to coursework assignments that are subject to examination, the internal examiner has the following responsibilities:

- notifying the students about the assignments prior to the commencement of the work, giving dates when such coursework should be submitted

- ensuring that secure systems are in place for the submission and receipt of coursework and that information on the procedures to be followed by students in this regard is communicated to students

- ensuring that appropriate criteria are established to assess the coursework and that examination procedures and standards correspond to best practice

• giving students unambiguous information on the consequences of late submission of coursework.

External examiners are most usually employed in respect of the final year examinations of a course, in order to provide an objective peer judgement on the standards achieved at the completion of the course. Each external examiner is usually appointed for a limited period, three years or the normal duration of the course. Frequently there may be more than one external examiner appointed, depending on the number of students and the number of specialisms covered in the course.

Nominations for external examiners are first made by the course committee and endorsed by the head of department, who informally consults with the nominee to ascertain their willingness and availability to serve as an external examiner. The nomination is approved by the academic council, generally some six months in advance of the date of the first examination at which the external examiner is required to act.

An external examiner should normally hold academic or professional qualifications similar to or higher than the award from the course to be examined. They should be of some eminence in the relevant academic field and/or the professional practice of the discipline. The head of department or their nominee is normally the sole contact person between the institution and the external examiner in relation to examination matters.

When the appointment of an external examiner is confirmed, the institution formally notifies them, providing details of the appointment, together with a range of briefing documents including the approved course document, previous examination papers and schedules for the forthcoming examinations and examination boards. These briefing documents should also contain information about the tasks of external examiners relative to draft examination papers, examination scripts, project reports, oral examinations and examination boards and any other relevant information. This liaison with the external examiner is carried out at the earliest possible stage by the head of department, to enable the external examiner to optimally plan for and fulfil the duties involved.

The external examiner reviews draft examination papers, including sample answers and marking schemes and provides comments on these to the head of department.

After the examination scripts have been marked, the external examiner visits the institution. They examine a representative sample of the candidates' marked examination scripts and/or other examination materials, such as candidates' assessed coursework, and may interview candidates when this is considered appropriate. The external examiners are not employed for the purposes of directly examining or marking the work of candidates, but rather for monitoring the examination process.

The internal and external examiners, in consultation with the head of department, normally agree the marks to be presented to the examination board. The external examiner attends the examination board meeting where the overall results for the candidates are decided.

The ultimate function of the external examiner is to ensure that the results achieved by each candidate in the overall examination are appropriate, judged by their performance, while bearing in mind the need for equity in examination, the level of the award, the objectives and nature of the course and the appropriate national and international standards which prevail in the discipline.

Each year, at the end of the examination process the external examiner presents a written report on the general standards reached by the candidates, giving comments on the overall conduct of the course and examinations and making suggestions for improvements.

The invigilation of written and practical examinations requires special attention.

Before candidates are admitted to the examination room the invigilator must ensure that the room has been set out with the materials required for the particular examination(s) to be held and that a clock is clearly visible to each candidate. Only candidates in possession of examination admission documentation should be permitted into the examination room and each should sign the attendance form and sit in their designated place. No unauthorised materials such as computing equipment, electronic organisers, programmable calculators, mobile phones, pagers, radios, tape recorders, books, notes, papers, drawings or other materials may normally be brought into the examination room.

The invigilator supplies any authorised materials to the candidates — examination papers, answer books, tables, etc. — and ensures that candidates are in possession of the correct examination papers before announcing the start of the examination. During the examination the candidates must be constantly supervised to ensure that they do not engage in unfair practice or activity likely to cause disturbance to other candidates. In the event of any query from a candidate concerning an examination paper the invigilator refers this to the examinations office for resolution by the internal examiner. Any clarification or correction provided is brought to the attention of all relevant candidates. The invigilator records any such matters in a report that is subsequently brought to the attention of the examination board.

The invigilator also implements the rules relative to candidates who leave the examination room during any period of the examination either without or with permission. In either case the invigilator records the event and the candidate's examination number. In the case where a candidate leaves without permission, such a candidate may not be readmitted during that examination. Where a candidate is given permission to leave the examination room for personal needs, or because of becoming distressed or ill, she/he must be accompanied at all times by an invigilator. If such a candidate is able to continue with the examination after a period of time has passed, a time extension equal to the period of absence from the examination room may be granted at the discretion of the examinations secretary.

Normally, no candidate is admitted to the examination room more than one half hour after the start of the examination. In exceptional circumstances, and provided that no other candidate sitting the same paper has withdrawn and left the examination room, a candidate may be admitted later, at the discretion of the examinations secretary. In such circumstances extra time is not normally allowed.

The invigilator announces the end of the examination period. She/he ensures that candidates stop writing when instructed to do so and submit all answer books and other materials for examination. The invigilator ensures that candidates remain seated while the scripts and other materials are being collected. They record the number of scripts submitted by each candidate and complete the invigilator's report. All of the candidates' scripts, all surplus unused answer books, examination question papers and other materials, together with the attendance sheet and the invigilator's report are then returned to the examinations office.

The internal examiner is required to mark anonymously each candidate's script, ensuring that the marks awarded are written clearly on the script, that they accord with those set out in the approved marking scheme and that all attempted questions are marked. They must also ensure that the marks awarded are transferred accurately to summary sheets, in preparation for the examination board. These are two stages when errors can easily arise and it is highly advisable that a team of colleagues is nominated within the department to check and recheck that the scripts are fully marked and that the marks have been correctly transferred.

The examination of coursework undertaken during the course — laboratory work, essays, projects and other assignments — presents other challenges. It is essential that the assignments to be examined and the submission dates, including penalties for late submission, be notified clearly to students in ample time. The actual submission also needs to be carefully recorded as well as any backup procedures. The internal examiner is required to establish appropriate examination criteria and procedures for such coursework which correspond to the best practice in the relevant discipline.

Breaches in examination rules, abuses and unfair practices by candidates in written examinations and assigned work, such as plagiarism and copying other persons' work, need to be specified carefully, together with the resulting penalties.

The examination board determines the results for the overall examination process for a given year or stage of a course, preparatory to the candidate being allowed to proceed to the next stage or year or to be given the final award of the course. The membership of the examination board must be clearly defined to include, typically:

- all internal and external examiners duly appointed for the course
- all heads of department involved with the course
- the head of faculty or their representative, usually acting as chairperson
- any approved representative of an external body, as observer
- a representative of the examinations office, as observer.

A quorum should be established and only members of the examination board may attend its meeting(s). The head of faculty may excuse a member from attending and nominate a replacement. All members attending duly sign the attendance sheet and undertake to maintain the strict confidentiality of the discussions at the meeting(s) of the examination board and within the examination process in general, in relation to individual candidates, elements of the examination and individual examiners. Only heads of department and their nominated representatives may discuss details of the examination results of individual candidates with the candidates concerned. They may not discuss them with third parties who are not members of the examination board.

The examination board is guided by the general institutional examination regulations, the specific regulations for the course as specified in the approved course document and the principles of natural justice. Any special circumstances that might have an influence on a candidate's performance and have been notified in writing to the authorities of the institution must be brought to the attention of the examination board. The board generally aims to reach its decisions by consensus, but if this is not possible, a majority vote, including one in which the chairperson may exercise a casting vote, determines the decision in any case.

Candidates are notified in the clearest possible way of the results of the deliberations of the examination board, including the overall result, the marks for individual subject elements and any requirements for reexamination. This may be done by public notice, but must be done in writing for each candidate as soon as possible after the examination board.

Examination results are one of the clearest measures of the success of a course and its delivery and are therefore a key aspect of quality assurance. It is vital that the responsible heads of department and the course committee systematically consider the results to derive the main lessons for use in planning course improvements.

The head of department, in consultation with the course committee, is responsible for preparing a summary report on the examination results, to give the following details, where applicable, in respect of each stage or year of the course and in respect of both female and male students:

- number of students registered
- number of candidates enrolled for the examination

- number who presented for examination
- overall number who passed
- number who achieved each honours grade
- number who achieved a pass grade
- number who gained exemptions and related credits
- number ineligible to continue
- subjects and subject components with average marks above overall average, with comments and explanations
- subjects and subject components with average marks below overall average with comments and explanations
- comments on results and comparison with previous years/stages and with comparable courses in the faculty.

The external examiner makes a formal written report to the faculty on the overall examination process, as soon as possible after the examination board meeting. This report should contain comments and suggestions on each of the following areas:

- presentation and timeliness of the draft examination papers
- structure, organisation, balance and standard of the examination papers
- marking of the examination papers, projects and other written presentations
- overall performance of the candidates, particularly in comparison with their peers nationally and internationally
- academic standards achieved by the candidates
- weaknesses evident in the examinations or course
- recommendations to improve the organisation and administration of the examination system
- other suggestions and recommendations for the course committee
- suggestions and recommendations to the institution
- any other comments.

The external examiner's report is a key element of peer judgement on the course and hence of academic quality assurance. It is returned to the faculty head who considers any issues of immediate concern that should be resolved by the faculty authorities and circulates copies to the head(s) of department involved with the course and to the chairperson of the course committee for appropriate action. The key points and recommendations should be discussed by the course committee and included in the annual monitoring report on the course.

A candidate who breaches the examination regulations or who attempts to procure such a breach through cheating, plagiarism, misrepresentation, bribery, falsification, impersonation and other forms of deception, including the possession of examination papers in advance of the examination, is subject to disciplinary procedures. A breach of regulations constituting unfair practice may be detected during the examination of any coursework for which credit is obtained, during invigilated examinations or during the marking of written examination scripts.

The procedures for reporting and subsequently processing and penalising such breaches of examination regulations must be fully documented and made available to all members of staff and to all students at first registration. These procedures must be transparent and guided by the principles of natural justice.

It is essential that the institution has clear and well publicised procedures for candidates to appeal the decision of an examination board. It is desirable that these procedures allow for an appeal to be resolved as early as possible and at as low a level in the organisation as possible. Thus a candidate considering an appeal should initially discuss the issue(s) with the head of department.

The valid bases for an appeal are generally one or more of the following grounds, where it is claimed that:

• the examination regulations of the institution, either general or specific to the course, were not properly implemented

• circumstances arose which may not have been covered by the examination regulations

• compassionate circumstances exist which relate to a candidate's examination situation.

ANNUAL MONITORING REPORT

In order to provide regular academic quality assurance on each course and to facilitate the course committee in considering the operation of the course and continuously improving it, an annual monitoring report on the functioning of the course in the previous academic year is prepared by the course committee and submitted through the head of department to the faculty authorities during the first term of each academic year.

The purpose of the annual monitoring report is to critically evaluate the course and its delivery and to ensure that academic standards are maintained and an active programme of development and improvement for the course is put in place. It allows the course committee to review the continued relevance of the course in the light of external developments in technology and in society. It provides an opportunity to assess the effectiveness of the continuous monitoring of the course throughout the academic year and implement corrective measures and other course improvements and modifications. It also allows the course committee to up-date the student handbook for the course.

The main elements of the annual monitoring report on the course are the examination results prepared in respect of each year of the course, the external examiners' reports and the course monitoring or quality ratings.

An extract of the key points of the external examiner's report together with a copy of the report by the head of department on the overall examination results for the course, with comments by the faculty head, constitutes the first part of the annual monitoring report.

The course committee carries out the other part of the annual course monitoring and quality rating for the course by accumulating the following data, observations and recommendations about the course:

- a summary of the recommendations of the previous annual report (or five-yearly review) and the subsequent actions on the key recommendations, as inserted in the approved course document

- performance indicators for the year or stage, giving target and actual student numbers enrolled, student to staff ratio figures, significant developments and factors affecting the course during the academic year, summary highlights of examination statistics, pass, fail, retention or other numbers, details of the placement of graduates and a summary of feedback from the students and staff

- the key comments of the external examiners in their reports

- an overview of the key issues affecting the course delivery, especially those needing remedial attention, and the development plan for the coming academic year including an examination of the course delivery, weaknesses and corrective measures to be taken, measures to be taken arising from the student feedback and from recommendations of the external examiners, measures to be taken on resource issues and on related academic developments including recruitment, staff professional development, research and other scholary activities

- proposed modifications to the course, especially those involving changes in examination regulations, must be recorded accurately and included in the annual amendments to the approved course document

- quality ratings for key aspects of the course including staffing, accommodation, equipment, teaching standards, learning environment and job placement of graduates

- comments by the chairperson of the course committee about the effectiveness of the functioning of the course committee

- comments by the head of department on the report, the quality ratings assigned by the course committee and issues relating to the course development plan

- overall quality rating by the faculty board on the scale from very good to poor and comments by the faculty head.

The following are general guidelines to allocating quality ratings on the four-point scale, *very good, good, fair* and *poor*.

Very Good — The course has well integrated objectives and a well organised and directed teaching programme. The staff members are well qualified and highly motivated, some are engaged in relevant research and/or industrial collaboration and they have good quality office accommodation and facilities. The lecture rooms, laboratories and other student accommodation are of a high quality, well designed and with a range of appropriate projection, video and computer-based display methods available. Equipment and other resources are of an advanced standard and accessible to the students on the course. Classes in the course are characterised by good teaching at a demanding level with challenging and relevant student assignments. Students are deeply and intelligently involved, show evidence of thorough learning, including considerable self-learning and appropriate progression, and are provided with regular feedback on their progress and with advice and guidance based on their examinations and other coursework. The oral and written work of the students is generally of a high standard. Graduates of the course obtain immediate employment or embark on further studies.

Good — The course has many of the features above but possibly some negative features. There may be more part time teachers involved than is desirable, some staff may not be as up-to-date as desirable and their facilities may be limited. The teaching accommodation may have some limitations with lecture rooms that may be overcrowded and requisite resources may not always be adequate. There may be equipment shortages in some areas or some equipment may not be quite up-to-date. Teaching is above average but possibly not sharply focussed or integrated. Student response may be good but could be improved, there may be little self-learning occurring and there may be some weakness in students' oral and/or written work. Overall the course quality is healthy and gives students ample opportunities to progress in most areas of the course, but improvements may be slow. Some graduates of the course may feel that it has not equipped them fully to obtain relevant employment or may feel unprepared for further studies.

Fair — The course is at an adequate mainstream level of quality, with some weaknesses counterbalanced by strengths. Staff may be complacent and continue to present the course in a routine manner from one year to the next. Accommodation may be broadly acceptable but with some limitations in quantity and/or standard. There may be little advanced equipment available for student use. Teaching may not be student-centred and may concern mainly factual information, with content reliable and solid but uninspiring. The response and work of the students is adequate but mixed and only few students reach what might be estimated as their full potential. The learning environment may be characterised by lack of challenge. Graduates have some difficulty gaining employment. The course urgently requires a fundamental self-study and review.

Poor — The course has some critical weaknesses in conception, integration, delivery or resources. Many staff members may be complacent and are not striving to inspire. The accommodation and facilities available are deficient in some areas and teaching resources may be rather basic or primitive. Some teaching may be poorly conceived and organised and ill matched to the capabilities of some of the students. Objectives are vague or are not achieved. The pace is slow and there may be little encouragement or possibility of independent student learning. Standards achieved in student oral and written work are sometimes not adequate for the level of award. The learning environment tends to be routine and moribund. Graduates have difficulty in finding employment directly and often feel they must work for additional qualifications. The course should be terminated or overhauled completely.

The use of such ratings allows the year-to-year changes, improvements and disimprovements to be charted and highlighted.

The annual monitoring report is first considered within the department and approved by the head of department. To the extent possible within the resources and budget of the department, the measures and improvements recommended in the report should be approved and decided at this level.

The report is then forwarded to the faculty authorities who review the proposed actions to ensure they enhance the academic content of the course and its delivery. Where some measures proposed require additional resources, they should be considered by the faculty authorities who may decide to make such additional resources available.

The annual monitoring report, together with details of the specific measures taken and comments by the head of department and head of the faculty, is forwarded to academic council.

When the faculty authorities approve the annual monitoring report on the course, a copy is forwarded by the head of department to each external examiner for their information. In the case of externally accredited courses, the annual monitoring report may also be forwarded to the external accrediting organisation.

Each year academic council, generally through a sub-committee, considers in detail the course annual monitoring reports from across the institution. Following this consideration, this academic quality assurance sub-committee of academic council may from time to time meet representatives from a course committee or require a course committee or the faculty authorities to give special attention to particular issues raised during the annual monitoring process.

As a result of the annual monitoring report, which might entail some consideration of developments in the profession and related industries, modifications to the course may be proposed. If the faculty authorities or academic council consider that any proposed course modifications are substantial, they may decide that a full or partial course review is necessary and request the faculty head to initiate such a process.

All modifications made to a course, or to the curriculum or examination regulations of any subject component, as a result of the annual monitoring report, must be documented. Copies of the amendments to the course document should be forwarded to the head of department, faculty head, faculty library and academic council in advance of the commencement of the next academic year. The amended course document then becomes the approved course document.

PERIODIC CRITICAL SELF-EVALUATION AND REVIEW

Each course conducted within an institution should be subject to periodic review, normally on a five-yearly cycle or more frequently as required by the academic council, faculty authorities or course committee. These five-yearly reviews are an opportunity for the course committee and course team to fundamentally reappraise the course and make major modifications to it, where considered appropriate.

If major modifications to a course are being proposed, the course committee should at an early stage consult the faculty authorities to obtain approval for such course modifications. In some cases, because of the extensive nature of proposed modifications, with serious implications in relation to resources and/or other programmes in the faculty, it may be necessary for the faculty authorities to obtain full course planning approval from the institution's authorities.

The main process involved in the review of a course is the fundamental, critical self-study or self-analysis and reappraisal of all aspects of the course by the course committee. This self-study is designed to help the course committee to improve the course. It should be a fundamental and comprehensive review, derived at least partly from the annual monitoring reports and quality ratings of the course for the period since the initial validation or the previous periodic review, but also from a study of developments in the discipline, in industry and society. It is an evaluation of the effectiveness of various aspects of the course, giving due recognition to problem areas as well as strengths and achievements. The self-study results in a thorough but concise report that aims to be an objective statement of the views of the course committee on the overall quality of the teaching and learning on the course and how it is to be developed.

The following aspects of the course should be addressed in the critical self-study report:

- aims and objectives of the course and its continuing relevance to the aims of the department, faculty and institution, relevant industrial, commercial and professional developments, impact of government and EU policies and regulations, job placement of graduates and feedback from employers

- admission requirements and standards of those admitted, intake policy and procedures, transfers into the course at advanced stages, mature students and numbers progressing through the course

- course structure and content, student workload, course delivery, optional subjects and elements and teaching techniques

- accommodation for course, teaching facilities and resources, library, IT and other learning resources

- technical and administrative support

- student placement for work experience and international student exchanges

- examinations, examination results, external examiners' reports, arrangements for annual monitoring and quality ratings

- membership of course committee, its operation, year co-ordinators and tutors, course advisory board, student handbook and other information channels to students, feedback from students and relevant student societies

- staff members teaching on course, their qualifications, involvement in research and scholarly activities and achievements, staff professional development, international staff exchanges, research underpinning the course and professional and industrial involvement

- outcome of the previous course development plan.

Details of major enhancements to the course arising from the reappraisal should be clearly indicated together with the rationale for introducing them. In the same context a medium term course development plan should also be elaborated, comprising the following aspects:

• detailed plans for the future development of course, giving time-scale

• staff professional development plans

• teaching and learning enhancement plans

• plans for improved annual monitoring of the course.

This self-study report is prepared by the course committee, but should draw from consultation with the course team, the staff members involved in teaching the course who are generally most aware of the strengths and weaknesses of the course. In preparing the self-study, the course committee consults with students and graduates of the course, industrialists and business people, government and other external organisations as appropriate. The self-study process therefore presents an ideal opportunity for those delivering the course to enhance its quality and delivery and indeed to impress their general ownership and identity on it.

The self-study also enables the review panel to highlight key areas for attention during the review event and facilitates the subsequent work of the faculty authorities in monitoring the implementation of the recommendations of the review panel.

The documentation required for a review event includes the written critical self-study and the proposed new course document, as described earlier in relation to the validation process. This course document should clearly incorporate the considerations and recommendations that emerged from the self-study process. The course committee may supply any other documentation deemed useful for the review event.

These documents are submitted for endorsement to the heads of department involved and the head of any external collaborating organisation. They are then forwarded to the faculty authorities, who review the course documentation submitted in a manner similar to their consideration of the documentation submitted for a validation event, described earlier. When they approve the course documentation, they advise the academic council of their views and request that a review panel be formed and that a review event be organised.

The main external peer review section of the review is carried out by a review panel which is required to make an impartial judgement on the continued maintenance of the overall standard of the course and on its acceptability for the award in question, when compared with similar courses elsewhere in Ireland and/or internationally.

The academic council, in consultation with the faculty authorities, is responsible for constituting the review panel, which is typically similar in composition to a validation panel as described previously. A candidate for membership of a review panel who has served as an external examiner on the course should have ended their external examinership at least two years before the review event.

In order to complete its work, the review panel visits the faculty to review the course documentation, discuss the course with the course committee, students and graduates of the course and view the facilities available for conducting the course. The review event typically has a timetable similar to a validation event.

The general issues considered and evaluated by a review panel encompass all of the issues considered by a validation panel but with an emphasis on the following aspects of the internal review:

- quality and comprehensiveness of the self-study of the course

- principles and philosophy underpinning the self-study and their relevance to the course

- evidence of course improvements in the annual monitoring and quality rating reports

- logic of the detailed recommendations arising from the self-study

- appropriateness of the proposed changes to the course to fulfil these recommendations

- overall health of the course and the procedures for academic quality assurance within it.

The review panel focuses mainly on the critical self-study report prepared by the course committee and views the revised course document, mainly to ensure that there is correlation between the conclusions of the self-study and the new course document and that any significant changes proposed are appropriate.

At the end of the review visit, the chairperson of the review panel may provide an oral presentation of the findings and conclusions of the panel to the faculty head, head of department and chairperson of the course committee.

The review panel prepares a written report, following the format of a course validation report. This report may indicate continuing approval of the course, make recommendations for modifying the course or set out special conditions for continuing approval. The confirmed and endorsed report is forwarded to the faculty head.

Consideration of the review panel report at course committee, department and faculty authority levels follows the same pattern described earlier for a validation panel report.

TERMINATION OF A COURSE

An approved course may normally be discontinued only with the approval of the academic council on the recommendation of the faculty authorities and the executive authorities of the institution.

Where an approved course does not operate for two years due to lack of student demand or lack of resources, its period of approval should lapse unless the reasons for the non-operation of the course have had prior acceptance from the faculty authorities. If the course approval lapses in this way, the head of department should be required to resubmit the course for validation and approval before it is offered again.

SUMMARY

The continuing assurance of quality in a course or programme requires the constant application of internal critical and honest peer review as well as regular input of external peer comments and recommendations, especially at key stages in the delivery of the course. The course team needs to maintain a steady vigilance over external academic and societal developments as well as a steady drive to enhance all aspects of the course, especially the weakest aspects.

CHAPTER SEVEN

Guidelines for the Assurance of Quality in Postgraduate Research — Project Planning and Student Recruitment

Research is that mode of teaching and learning least well-defined and possibly least well-understood, even by its practitioners. Achieving a postgraduate degree through research has been described as "the academic equivalent of scaling an unclimbed peak".[1] Of its nature it is a venture into the relatively unknown.

Research may be original investigation to gain knowledge and understanding. It may be relevant to the needs of industry, commerce and enterprise, of education itself and of the public and voluntary sectors. It may involve invention and development of ideas, images, performances and artefacts and/or designs with new insights. It may lead to new developments and new applications of ideas, new and improved materials, devices, products and processes.

Postgraduate research work leading to a postgraduate award is normally undertaken by a postgraduate student in a topic closely related to their undergraduate discipline or industrial or professional work experience. The work is carried out under the supervision and guidance of at least one full-time member of staff of the institution, who is qualified and experienced in the field involved. While an institution may consider research project proposals in any of the discipline areas of its constituent departments, the research supervisors on the staff, each with their expertise and commitment, are the key people in determining the feasibility of the programmes of research work undertaken.

---

[1] Cryer, P, *The Research Student's Guide to Success* (Buckingham: Open University Press) 1996.

POSTGRADUATE DEGREES AND OTHER AWARDS THROUGH RESEARCH

In general a student may register in a higher education institution on a research programme leading to a postgraduate diploma (research), a master's degree or a doctoral degree.

Quality and quality assurance in postgraduate research are the responsibility of the academic council, as is the case for undergraduate academic programmes. A postgraduate research committee is appointed by the academic council with general terms of reference and responsibilities in relation to ensuring quality assurance in postgraduate research.[2]

The main quality assurance functions of the postgraduate research committee, carried out in close consultation with the relevant faculty authorities, heads of department and research supervisors, are to:

- recommend to academic council the admission of applicants to each of the registers of postgraduate students of the institution — postgraduate diploma (by research), master's degree and doctoral degree registers

- oversee the approval of postgraduate research projects and endorse the management and supervision arrangements for postgraduate research students

- monitor the progress of those entered on each of the registers of postgraduate students

- regulate and approve transfers between the three registers

- prescribe and ensure the format and layout of final theses

- prescribe and administer examination processes in relation to theses, oral examinations and other forms of examination and assessment as may be considered appropriate to postgraduate research study

- generally make recommendations to the academic council on matters pertaining to the conduct of postgraduate studies by research.

PROJECT DESIGN AND PLANNING

The postgraduate research committee is empowered to accept proposals for research study over the full range of academic disciplines and scholarship catered for within the institution. Proposals relating to the various applied

---

[2] Dublin Institute of Technology, *Regulations for Postgraduate Study by Research* (Dublin) 2nd edition, 1997; Higher Education Quality Council, *Guidelines on the Quality Assurance of Research Degrees* (London) 1996.

areas of the institution's expertise and involvement, with industrial, commercial, social, professional and/or artistic dimensions may be considered. Similarly proposals for collaborative, interdisciplinary research studies involving industrial, commercial, professional and governmental organisations and other educational institutions, both within Ireland and elsewhere in the EU, may also emerge.

The most usual source of a research project proposal is an individual member of staff, who is normally the prime supervisor of the project. A project may also arise out of collaboration between staff members, from industrial co-operation or from the interests of a prospective postgraduate student. At the proposal stage it is essential that the project proposer(s) or supervisor(s) set out a plan of the project, seeking the resources required, with the following features:

- outline of the technical and other aims of the project

- the resources available and those required (personnel, space, equipment, finances) to carry out the project in the time required

- the responsibilities of the supervisor(s), postgraduate student(s) and any other personnel involved

- the reporting arrangements to head of department, faculty authorities, industrial and other partners and funding agencies.

At departmental level it is essential that the project be assessed according to a number of criteria — can the project be carried out with the equipment and budget available, in the accommodation available and in the time available; does the staff member involved possess the requisite academic background required to the level required or should additional supervision be provided; can the department continue to provide adequate supervision in the event of the nominated supervisor becoming ill or leaving the institution; and finally can the project be formulated and directed in such a way as to offer the depth and breadth of intellectual and academic challenge appropriate to the level of postgraduate award proposed?

The experience and track record of the proposed supervisor(s) are key elements in establishing the feasibility of a proposed project. The head of department should attest to the general fulfilment of all of these criteria before a project is approved and a postgraduate student recruited to work on it. At this stage also, the project supervisor should set out a more detailed plan of the project than done at the earlier proposal stage, based on resources made available, with the following features:

- the personnel, training, physical and technical objectives, with specific landmark achievements and targets, by each month

- the broad expenditures and financial targets, by each month

- the duties of the supervisor(s), postgraduate student(s) and any other personnel involved

- the reporting arrangements to supervisor, head of department, department and faculty seminars, postgraduate research office, industrial and other partners and funding agencies.

Changes in the plan in the light of experience and progress on the project must be included later in monthly, quarterly, mid-year and annual reports.

POSTGRADUATE STUDENT RECRUITMENT AND REGISTRATION

In order to be entered in the postgraduate diploma (research) register, an applicant must possess, as a minimum, the equivalent of a pass degree in a relevant subject from a recognised higher education institution and must have demonstrated an aptitude and ability to carry out research work of an appropriate level. Relevant work experience may be taken into account in determining acceptability.

To qualify for direct entry to the master's degree register, an applicant is normally required to possess at least the equivalent of a second class honours primary degree in a relevant subject from a recognised academic institution. Relevant work experience and demonstrated capacity to carry out the research work may also be taken into account in determining acceptability. Postgraduate students already on the postgraduate diploma (research) register and progressing satisfactorily are usually entitled to apply for transfer to the master's degree register.

Direct entry to the doctoral degree register is normally restricted to applicants who already possess a master's degree in an area related to that of their proposed research. Postgraduate students already on the master's degree register and working successfully at an appropriate level may apply for transfer to the doctoral degree register.

It is generally desirable for an applicant to visit and consult with the head of the relevant department within the institution before making a formal application for registration. This contact allows thorough discussion of the proposed research project between the prospective postgraduate student and the prospective supervisor(s). It also facilitates discussion of supervision and funding arrangements and the availability of laboratory and other resources required. If it is proposed that some or all of the work be carried out in a location external to the institution, details of the facilities to be externally provided and the arrangements for suitable supervision may be examined. If the applicant has relevant research, industrial, professional or other practical work experience, these discussions may help the prospective supervisor(s) and the relevant head of department to evaluate that work experience as part of the prerequisites for entry. These discussions should also clarify the training and skills that the prospective postgraduate student may need to acquire in order to carry out the research work. Furthermore, such discussions will help to clarify for the applicant the appropriate postgraduate register for which the application should be made.

An applicant for postgraduate study by research in the institution must normally provide the postgraduate research committee with an official transcript of their undergraduate academic results, photocopies of their degree(s) and/or any other diploma(s) and at least two references in support of the application. The referees selected should have personal knowledge of the applicant and their academic qualifications and/or other relevant experience. They should be from either an academic or industrial or commercial background. Referees are requested to provide, in confidence, information and evaluations, attesting to the applicant's aptitude and fitness for postgraduate research in the particular discipline.

The postgraduate research committee assesses each application to ensure that:

- the applicant possesses or will possess the required qualifications, or their equivalent, prior to registration

- the proposed research programme of work is appropriate for the postgraduate award for which the applicant wishes to register

- the institution can provide the academic expertise, facilities and resources required for the proposed research programme

- provision has been made for adequate supervision of the proposed research programme.

As mentioned previously, academic supervision is central to the successful completion of postgraduate research work. Supervisor(s) play a key role in devising research projects, guiding the postgraduate student throughout their work, determining the specific direction of the research in conjunction with the student, setting appropriate academic standards to be attained by the student and assessing when they achieve them. It is highly desirable that more than one supervisor be appointed to provide the supervision of the postgraduate research student. This can be beneficial for the student who can obtain advice from more than one person on the project, for the supervisors who carry a shared burden and together can make more progress on the project than can one alone, and for the institution which is not compromised if a supervisor leaves during the project.

The appointment of each academic supervisor is made by the postgraduate research committee in consultation with the head of department in which the research work is primarily to be undertaken and with the approval of the proposed supervisor. The supervisor should normally be a full time member of staff of that department and should possess appropriate expertise in the area of the proposed research work. A supervisor should normally hold a qualification at least equivalent to the award being sought by the postgraduate student under supervision.

Additionally the supervisor should possess prior experience of successful postgraduate research supervision at the level of the award being sought by the applicant. If a proposed supervisor does not have this requisite experience, they may be appointed as a supervisor but a suitably experienced additional advisory or mentoring supervisor should also be appointed by the postgraduate research committee, in consultation with the original supervisor and the head of department. If a full time staff member is not available to act as advisory supervisor, arrangements must be made with an experienced staff member from another academic institution to serve as the advisory supervisor. In the conduct and management of the project the original supervisor may provide the bulk of the day-to-day supervision of the postgraduate student's work, but under the general guidance of the advisory supervisor who takes overall and ultimate academic responsibility for the work and its quality.

This approach helps to assure the quality of the research work and its supervision. It is also a form of apprenticeship and staff development for research supervisors which helps to minimise the risks of inadequate supervision for the postgraduate student and indeed for the institution itself.

Where research work is interdisciplinary, involving more than one department of the institution or is done in collaboration with an external organisation, a second (or third) supervisor, nominated by the head of the second department or by the external organisation, may be appointed by the postgraduate research committee, with the approval of the head of department primarily responsible and of the other (original and advisory) supervisors. This supervisor is expected to act in collaboration with the advisory and proposing supervisor(s).

The postgraduate research committee should have the right to change supervision arrangements where necessary, in consultation with the head of department, with the approval of academic council.

Before final acceptance or rejection of an application, formal acceptance of the proposed supervision arrangements by the supervisor(s) and the responsible head of department should be required. This acceptance must be endorsed by the head of department, who thereby confirms that the project is of an adequate standard, the planning and supervision arrangements are satisfactory, the requisite facilities and resources are available for the proposed programme of work and the applicant is appropriately prepared to undertake the research programme.

The decision of the postgraduate research committee is communicated in writing to the applicant, to the supervisor(s) and to the head of department concerned. If the decision is to reject the application, the grounds for rejection are included in this communication. The decision and any grounds for rejection are formally submitted to academic council for approval.

Registration takes place as soon as possible after approval has been given and prior to the agreed commencement date of the research programme.

The period of registration is normally one academic year, with annual renewal of registration required. Renewal of registration is approved by the postgraduate research committee only on the basis of satisfactory progress in the work. Evidence of such progress is provided by the postgraduate student and by the supervisor(s) in the form of progress reports submitted to the postgraduate research committee during the year of registration. Permission to renew registration is communicated to each postgraduate student and reregistration takes place at the start of the following academic year.

All students included in the postgraduate registers, whether full-time or part-time, are fully students of the institution and as such are entitled to the same rights and privileges as undergraduate students and equally are subject to the general conduct and discipline regulations of the institution. These postgraduate students must comply with the regulations for postgraduate studies by research and in particular the regulations for the postgraduate award for which they are registered.

INDUCTION OF THE NEW POSTGRADUATE STUDENT

Postgraduate research is qualitatively different from most undergraduate programmes and the new postgraduate student must be helped to make the transition from the undergraduate approach to the mode of thought and work of postgraduate research.

It is of importance to introduce the new postgraduate student to the academic and social surroundings in which they are to function for the next two years or more and to consciously integrate them into that environment. This environment includes the department and faculty, the overall institution and, where appropriate, the city and its geographic hinterland. The induction process may be a mixture of workshop sessions shared by a number of new postgraduate students and sessions between the individual student and their supervisor(s). Amongst the aspects that are valuable to this induction process are the following:

- the research profile of the department, faculty and overall institution
- the postgraduate research regulations, including registration procedures and prerequisites
- office and laboratory accommodation, including access arrangements and research equipment availability
- education and training courses required

- specific training programme relating to the work of the project, research skills and techniques of the discipline
- background material about the specific project, research sources and literature
- library and IT facilities
- health, safety, legal and ethical information
- welfare arrangements
- research supervision arrangements, lines of responsibility, how to solve problems in relation to supervision
- reporting arrangements, including seminars and written reports.

SUMMARY

The foundation for successful, high quality postgraduate research is the thorough planning of and preparation for the research project by the supervisor and the department, coupled with the matching of the postgraduate student to the project work plan.

CHAPTER EIGHT

Guidelines for the Assurance of Quality in Postgraduate Research — Progressing the Research Work to Completion

After a postgraduate student has been recruited and inducted into a department, it is of the greatest importance that the research project work be steadily progressed to an appropriate depth and extent for the postgraduate award in question, within a reasonable time duration. This requires a unique and continuous collaboration between the postgraduate student, the supervisor(s) and the head of department.

RESPONSIBILITIES OF THE COLLABORATORS

Within this collaboration, each of the parties carries a range of mutual responsibilities.

The supervisor has a range of duties and responsibilities in overseeing the progress of the postgraduate student's research work. Specifically the supervisor is required to:

- provide the student with guidance to and a critique of the background literature on the project

- ensure that the student undergoes any necessary training in research skills and techniques, including all safety, ethical and legal aspects of the work

- arrange a regular schedule of meetings with the postgraduate student to provide advice on the topic of the research and on the work to be undertaken, maintain a permanent record of these meetings in a logbook format and assess and note the progress of the research

- require regular written reports from the student in order to monitor the progress of the work and be able to provide constructive criticism

- clearly identify inadequacies in the work of the student at as early a stage as possible, in order to maintain appropriate standards and allow adequate time for reorientation and correction

- where appropriate, co-operate and liaise closely with any other supervisor(s) involved in the research
- ensure that the research is conducted within the ethical standards of the institution, the discipline and any other appropriate external agencies
- advise the postgraduate research committee on the student's progress, through submitting regular progress reports
- refer the student to a professional counsellor, if necessary, in relation to problems external to the research
- recommend that the student be permitted to transfer from the postgraduate diploma (research) register to the master's degree register and participate in the transfer examination
- recommend that the student be permitted to transfer from the master's degree register to the doctoral degree register and participate in the transfer examination
- advise the student when work has reached an appropriate completion stage such that the thesis may be written and give approval for the preparation of the thesis
- advise the student on the format and lay-out of the thesis
- endorse the notice of intention to submit the thesis, indicating that the student is eligible to do so
- advise on the nomination of two external examiners for the examination of the thesis and the possible oral examination of the candidate for the relevant award
- assist the head of department in the nomination of an internal examiner for the examination of the thesis and the possible oral examination of the student
- read the thesis material in both proof and final form, before it is formally submitted for examination and provide the postgraduate research committee with a general commentary on the work and a report on the adequacy of the thesis for the award in question
- arrange if possible for the thesis to be independently read, evaluated and commented on by a colleague prior to the formal submission
- agree, if possible, with the student when the thesis is suitable for submission
- attend any oral examination of the candidate required by the examiners.

The duties of the advisory or mentoring supervisor, when appointed with an inexperienced supervisor, are to:

- provide guidance and assistance to the original proposing supervisor(s) in the planning of the research programme and ensuring the attainment and maintenance of an appropriate academic standard in the work being undertaken

- liaise with the postgraduate student and the proposing supervisor(s)

- help to resolve difficulties and advise on procedures throughout the work

- advise the postgraduate research committee on the progress of the student, through submitting regular progress reports

- read and evaluate the thesis in both draft and final form, before it is submitted for examination

- reach agreement with the proposing supervisor(s) on the nomination of suitable external examiners and assist the head of department in the nomination of a suitable internal examiner

- agree, if possible, with the student that the thesis is suitable for submission.

The head of department acts on behalf of the institution and is required to:

- approve the appointment of the supervisor(s), ensure the availability of the required facilities and approve the acceptance of an applicant for postgraduate study by research

- advise the postgraduate research committee on the appointment of an advisory supervisor with the proposing supervisor in the case of the latter not possessing an appropriate postgraduate qualification or not having experience of successful postgraduate research supervision at the appropriate level

- approve the supervisors' regular reports on the progress of the work before their submission to the postgraduate research committee

- in relation to an application from a student for transfer from the postgraduate diploma (research) register to the master's degree register, advise the postgraduate research committee on the appointment of a transfer examiner

- in relation to an application from a student for transfer from the master's degree register to the doctoral degree register, to advise the postgraduate research committee on the appointment of a transfer examiner

- approve a decision by a student to transfer from one register to a lower register and notify the postgraduate research committee of this decision

- endorse the three months' notice of intention to submit a postgraduate diploma (research), master's or doctoral thesis, indicating that the student is eligible to do so

- with the assistance of the supervisor(s), propose the nominations of two appropriate external examiners and one internal examiner for the final examination process for each award
- provide the postgraduate research committee with a general commentary on the research work and an assessment report on the suitability of the thesis for the award sought.

The registered postgraduate student is required to:

- participate fully in the induction process
- agree with the appointed supervisor(s) on a programme for the proposed research and on the nature and extent of guidance required
- agree a regular schedule of meetings with the supervisor(s), including the advisory supervisor where appointed, and contribute to maintaining a permanent record or logbook of these meetings
- undertake any necessary courses and training as required by the research supervisor(s)
- inform the supervisor(s) of significant problems and difficulties as early as possible
- maintain progress on a work schedule agreed in consultation with the supervisor(s)
- conduct the research within the safety and ethical standards of the institution and of any other appropriate external agencies
- present written material on the work being undertaken as required by the supervisor(s)
- provide regular progress reports
- reach agreement with the supervisor(s) on any decision to apply for transfer to a higher register
- notify the supervisor(s) about a decision to seek a transfer to a lower register
- agree with the supervisor(s) on a date for submission of the thesis
- give three months' notice of intention to submit a postgraduate diploma (research), master's or doctoral thesis to the postgraduate research committee
- decide, if possible with the agreement of the supervisor(s), that the thesis is suitable for submission.

MONITORING THE PROGRESS OF THE RESEARCH WORK[1]

At the very earliest preparatory stage in a postgraduate research project, it is essential that the postgraduate student and supervisor(s) establish clearly what the research project is meant to achieve and a timetable for the work. Intermediate steps along the way, and alternative and parallel steps if such are possible, should be agreed and put in writing. The main methodologies to be used, the problems and impediments to progress and the key landmarks or turning points in the work should be itemised and the skills and competencies required of the student — and hence the training they may require — should also be listed. This planning process can help the student and supervisor(s) to uncover the elements of novelty in the work, an aspect that is generally required in research leading to postgraduate degrees.

This process can then allow a first draft of a timetable for the main stages of the work to be drawn up. This will entail managing access to the facilities and resources required at the appropriate times in the work. It will also entail planning for progress reports and progress meetings between student and supervisor(s). It will also require agreement on the quantity of work and the level of performance needed in each stage of the research. The process also requires the review of the recent literature on the subject of the research to gain an appreciation of high level research work and good quality reports on such work.

In mapping out alternative approaches, it may be possible to devise preliminary experiments and investigations which, in turn, can help to determine the most productive and insightful approaches to be used. Such preliminary work can also allow the criteria for calibration, comparison and validation of the results of the project to be established.

The first draft plan and timetable serve as a guide to the early part of the project. But it must be reviewed and modified in the light of experience and the improved insight into the project which comes with doing the work and writing interim reports on it.

At the start of the research work it is essential that the postgraduate student become familiar with the overall context and theoretical framework of the proposed work, through reading reports and publications on earlier related work. Relatively recent papers in the literature and postgraduate theses are useful sources for this investigation. The internet is becoming extremely valuable as well in this respect and allows the student to communicate and

---

[1] Blaxter, L, C Hughes and M Tight, *How to Research* (Buckingham: Open University Press) 1996; Bell, J, *Doing your Research Project* (Buckingham: Open University Press) 2nd edition, 1993; Phillips, E M, and D S Pugh, *How to get a PhD: a Handbook for Students and Supervisors* (Buckingham: Open University Press) 2nd edition, 1994; O'Sullivan, B, *Personal Communication* (Dublin: Dublin Institute of Technology) 1999.

consult with many of the international workers in the field. Not only must the student read relatively widely around the subject, but she/he must also make notes and discuss findings with the supervisor. This library work helps to lay the foundations for the subsequent practical work and establishes its relevance to the broader field. It may also help to determine the more fruitful approaches to the basic problem, by clarifying the norms of the particular discipline, the limitations of the approaches available and the optimum techniques of analysis of measurements and data.

While every research project begins with a problem and with various levels of understanding of that problem by the supervisor(s) and student, the work itself is a process of continuously clarifying and redefining that problem. This can only be done properly through written reports by the student, which are then discussed with the supervisor(s) and other colleagues experienced in the subject matter. This is especially important where critical decisions or shifts of emphasis or approach must be made in the work.

As well as investigating the background to the project that may be available in the published literature, it may also be necessary to carry out a range of preliminary practical or laboratory investigations, to establish firm foundations for the approaches to be taken. Such practical investigations can provide insight into the viability and relative ease of different possible approaches. They can help the student to gain familiarity with the equipment and the analytical techniques to be used in the project. They facilitate definitive decisions on the methodology to be used and greater clarity on the scheduling of the work to be done.

Generally speaking, the progress of research work is neither smooth nor predictable. The outcome of each stage of the work may alter the priorities for the next stages. Above all it is vital for the postgraduate research student to work, take notes and report in a systematic manner. This will allow progress to be monitored and the encouragement that comes from progress to be brought to bear on the work. The goals for each stage, set in conjunction with the supervisor(s), should be realistic and attainable. The results of a piece of work may be positive or negative, but a negative result does not mean that the work and its results are invalid or without value. When a discrete stage of the work is completed, the report on it should be written and discussed with the supervisor(s).

The basic aim of postgraduate research is the production of a written thesis for examination for the award. Therefore learning to produce written reports is a fundamental task for the postgraduate student.[2] It is advisable that the student should undertake as a first written assignment before the end of the first month, the production of a thorough description of the theoretical and practical basis for the project and an outline of the work proposed.

---

[2] Creme, P and M R Lea, *Writing at University: a Guide for Students* (Buckingham: Open University Press) 1997.

Regular writing and submitting of reports are key features of research work. This provides valuable opportunities for clarifying the progress of the work and obtaining feedback from supervisor(s), other lecturing staff, fellow students and friends. It may be possible that a stage or section of the work would be appropriate to be written up for submission to a relevant peer reviewed journal. Such an outcome provides ample assurance about the appropriateness of the work for a postgraduate degree thesis.

Another vital aspect of academic life and peer review of research work is the relatively formal oral presentation of research findings at departmental seminars and the still more formal presentation of results at national and international conferences.

Progress reports, typically quarterly or bi-annually, are required to be completed and returned to the postgraduate research committee.

A progress report consists of one part completed independently by the postgraduate student and another completed independently by the supervisor(s). The student's part is required to provide a typewritten description of the work of about two or three pages at quarterly or mid-year stages and of a more comprehensive ten to twenty pages at the annual stage. This is appended to the basic formal report.

The postgraduate research committee considers each progress report. If a report is unsatisfactory, the postgraduate research committee may seek further clarification from the supervisor(s) and/or from the head of department, or may require a resubmission.

In order to renew registration for the continuation of the work in the subsequent academic year, the progress reports for the previous year must have been received and approved by the postgraduate research committee.

Having been at least one half-year full time (or equivalent) on the postgraduate diploma (research) register a student may, with the support of their supervisor(s), apply to the postgraduate research committee to transfer to the master's degree register. To do so, the supervisor(s) is required to obtain the endorsement of the head of department and submit the application to the postgraduate research committee. The student and supervisor(s) should give cogent reasons to support the transfer request.

In consultation with the head of department, the postgraduate research committee appoints a transfer examiner to assess the quality and progress of the student's research work to date as well as the proposed programme of work for the master's degree. This transfer examiner should have academic qualifications and expertise in an area related to the research being undertaken. They may be from the staff of the institution or from an external organisation. The transfer examiner, normally in the presence of the supervisor(s) and an independent chairperson nominated by the postgraduate research committee, conducts an oral examination of the student in order to assess their suitability for transfer to the master's degree register in the context of the proposed research programme. A written report on this evaluation, together with recommendations, is submitted to the postgraduate research committee.

Having been at least one year full time (or equivalent) on the master's degree register a student may, with the support of their supervisor(s) apply to the postgraduate research committee to transfer to the doctoral register. A transfer process similar to that described above is then followed.

The postgraduate research committee considers the application for transfer, together with the evaluation report and recommendations of the transfer examiner and either approves or rejects the application.

In the case of such a transfer being approved, the work already carried out by the student while on the lower register may be incorporated into the programme of work for the higher award, if this incorporation is recommended by the transfer examiner and approved by the postgraduate research committee.

The postgraduate research committee is required to provide in writing the reasons for a rejection to the student, the supervisor(s) and the head of department. The student, supervisor(s) and head of department, collectively or individually, may appeal such a rejection to academic council.

A postgraduate student may at any time, in consultation with their supervisor(s), decide to transfer to a lower register. The student should notify the supervisor(s) in writing of this decision. The supervisor then notifies the postgraduate research committee, which in turn alters the registration of the student.

The minimum duration of research work leading to the award of a postgraduate diploma (research), is normally one year full time or equivalent. The maximum duration is two years full time or equivalent.

The minimum duration of the work leading to the award of a master's degree, is normally one year full time or equivalent. The maximum duration is three years full time or equivalent.

The minimum duration of the work leading to the doctoral degree is normally two years full time or equivalent. The maximum duration in this case is four years full time or equivalent.

Irrespective of prescribed minimum and maximum periods of study, the quality and quantity of the research work undertaken and then presented in a thesis must be at a level appropriate to the award sought and in an area relevant to the faculty in which the work is undertaken. In making any decision to terminate and submit work for formal examination, a student must liaise closely with and be advised by the supervisor(s).

When the research work reaches an appropriate completion stage for the award in question, the thesis is produced and submitted for examination. Close and detailed discussion between the postgraduate student and the supervisor(s) is required to determine that the quantity and quality of the presented work is appropriate to the level of the award sought. They must be assured that sufficient measurements or observations have been made to draw useful conclusions from the work. At this stage also they must agree about the best method of presenting the work and its results in the thesis.

Normally, if the recommended practice of regularly writing reports on the work done is followed, the student will have written large amounts of the draft thesis, including numbers of individual chapters, at stages during the implementation of the work. In such circumstances the completion of the draft thesis need not be a daunting task or take a great deal of time. Nevertheless the provision of a reasonably quiet space in the department, close to laboratory, library and supervisor(s) is highly desirable for the most expeditious completion of the draft thesis.

THESIS

The regulations for postgraduate studies by research of an institution specify the format for the presentation of the thesis, appropriate for each level of award. The format specifications cover the following aspects of the thesis:

- language of the thesis
- declaration guaranteeing that the work is the candidate's own
- recommended format, length and presentation
- title page
- acknowledgements
- abstract
- table of contents
- use of photographs and diagrams
- use of footnotes and quotations
- specification of references
- length of thesis for each level of award
- declaration stating that copies submitted become the property of the institution
- declaration specifying the allowed access to the thesis
- issues concerning publication of material from thesis
- copyright matters.

Previously successful theses provide practical examples of how these specifications may be implemented. The postgraduate student should consult such theses at the earliest opportunity in the course of the work.

A postgraduate student is required to give three months' prior notice of submission of a postgraduate diploma (research) or master's or doctoral thesis to the postgraduate research committee. The notice should be appropriately completed by the student and the supervisor(s), endorsed by the head of department and forwarded to the postgraduate research committee. The student is required to be validly registered when giving this notice. When the committee receives the notice, the student becomes a candidate for the relevant postgraduate award and is so notified in writing.

The postgraduate research committee then appoints an external examiner, an internal examiner (or two external examiners, if no suitable internal examiner is available or a candidate is a full time member of staff of the institution) and possibly an independent chairperson of examiners to conduct the examination of the thesis and the oral examination of the candidate, where this is deemed desirable by the examiners.

Two persons of suitable academic standing are nominated by agreement between the supervisor(s) and the head of department as first and second choice external examiners. The head of department, in consultation with the supervisor(s), also nominates an internal examiner. Through a process of informal contact, the head of school should ascertain the willingness of the nominees to act in this capacity, if appointed, and their availability within a six week period after the intended submission date for the thesis.

An examiner is normally a person active in research, of some eminence in the broad field of the candidate's research, with academic qualifications at least of the level of the award in question and experience of successful postgraduate research supervision. A person possessing wide industrial or commercial experience in an area directly related to the topic of the candidate's research may also be considered for appointment, provided cogent reasons for the nomination are supplied. A brief CV of each such candidate should be supplied to the postgraduate research committee. The details provided should enable the postgraduate research committee to be assured that the nominees are academically or otherwise suitable and experienced to examine the thesis and the candidate for the postgraduate award in question.

The postgraduate research committee may choose two or three of the nominated persons to act as examiner(s). In cases where no suitable internal examiner is available or where the candidate is a full time member of staff of the institution, then two external examiners are normally appointed. The postgraduate research committee subsequently issues a formal written invitation to the selected examiner(s).

For the first submission of the thesis, three soft bound copies should be submitted. The copies of the thesis submitted are examined by the postgraduate studies office to check that they follow the rules of format and presentation set by the institution. If they do not follow these rules they are returned to the candidate for correction. Accepted copies of the thesis are transmitted to the nominated examiners for examination.

The overall examination consists of an examination of the thesis and, for a doctoral award, a mandatory oral examination of the candidate. In the case of a candidate for a lower award, an oral examination may be held where this is considered desirable by the examiners.

The thesis for the postgraduate diploma (by research) is a minor thesis that should show competence in the research methodology, knowledge of the context of the work and critical appreciation of the results achieved.

A master's thesis should broadly show independent thought and work by the candidate, a scholarly approach and a critical appreciation of the context and significance of the work undertaken.

A doctoral thesis should contain evidence of original, independent work of significance and should make an important contribution to the existing body of knowledge on the subject through new discoveries or interpretations. It should demonstrate the candidate's critical ability and their capacity to undertake further independent research.

In cases where the work carried out is part of a collaborative project, the thesis should clearly show the candidate's specific contribution and the extent of collaboration involved. It is essential that the candidate be judged on their work only.

When an oral examination of the candidate is required, the postgraduate research committee, in consultation with the supervisor(s) and the head of department, appoints a chairperson of examiners. The oral examination is convened by the chairperson of examiners and takes place as soon as possible after the examination of the thesis. The examiners interview the candidate in the presence of the chairperson. The supervisor(s) may also be present as observer(s) at the oral examination. The oral examination should allow the candidate to demonstrate that the work presented in the thesis is their own work, that they adequately understand the subject and appreciate the broader context and relevance of the work.

An examination report is completed by each of the examiners and forwarded to the postgraduate research office. The reports cover both thesis assessment and oral examination (if held) and each concludes with a recommendation from the examiner. The examiners should consult each other in order to reach a consensus, if possible. In the event that the examiners cannot agree, the recommendation of the external examiner is accepted.

The examiners may make one of the following recommendations:

- that the award be made with no corrections needed in the thesis

- that the thesis is acceptable for the award but that the candidate be permitted to withdraw the thesis for appropriate revision and resubmission at a later date for a higher award, a master's degree in the case of a postgraduate diploma (research) candidate or a doctoral degree in the case of a master's degree candidate

- that the award be made subject to the verified inclusion in the thesis of relatively minor corrections and specified revisions

- that the award not be made but that the candidate be allowed to resubmit the thesis subject to major corrections and/or major specified revisions, and that the candidate be required then to undergo an oral examination

- that the award not be made but that the candidate be recommended for a lower award, a master's degree in the case of a doctoral candidate and a postgraduate diploma (research) in the case of a master's degree candidate

- that the candidate be permitted to withdraw the thesis without prejudice or penalty

- that no award be made.

Each examiner should state clear reasons for their recommendation and provide a clear written statement of any changes, corrections and/or revisions required.

The postgraduate research committee considers the examination report for approval. The outcome at this stage is provisional and is notified as such to the candidate, supervisor(s) and head of department. The result is forwarded to the academic council for final approval. The decision of the academic council is the final result of the candidate's examination.

If corrections and/or revisions (major or minor) and resubmission of the thesis are required, the detailed recommendations are communicated to the candidate, supervisor(s) and head of department.

In the event of a candidate being recommended to withdraw a thesis for revision and resubmission at a later date for a higher award, such resubmission may not be made before the candidate has been on the appropriate postgraduate studies register for at least one year full time in the case of resubmission for a master's degree and for at least two years full time in the case of resubmission for a doctoral degree. Different external examiner(s) are normally appointed for the subsequent examination for the higher award.

In the event that the examiners recommend corrections and/or revisions, only one resubmission is allowed. This resubmission should normally be made. using the recommended format, within one calendar year of the date of the oral examination.

If the resubmitted thesis is one that has had relatively minor corrections and revisions made to it, a copy of the resubmitted thesis is forwarded to the internal examiner for examination. If, in the judgement of the internal examiner, the recommended corrections and revisions have been adequately incorporated, the internal examiner confirms this by signing the appropriate part of the examination report.

If the resubmitted thesis is one that has had major corrections and revisions made to it, copies of the resubmitted thesis are sent to the internal and external examiners for re-examination. If required by the examiners, the chairperson convenes an oral examination and the chairperson chairs a meeting of the examiners. Subsequently a new examination report is completed by each examiner, incorporating a unanimous recommendation from the examiners. The examiners should give clear reasons for their final recommendation, as part of their written report.

The postgraduate research committee considers the final examination report on the resubmitted thesis and may accept the report, modify it before accepting it or reject it.

The decision of the postgraduate research committee is submitted for approval by the academic council. The decision of the academic council is the final result.

If the provisional result of the examination process is that the award sought is not to be awarded, the candidate may appeal this result according to the academic appeals procedure outlined in Chapter 6. Such an appeal can only refer to the circumstances of the examination and not to the conduct and supervision of the project.

FEEDBACK FROM THE POSTGRADUATE STUDENT

The process of postgraduate research requires regular interactions between the student, the supervisor(s), the head of department and the postgraduate research committee. Every effort should be made at all levels to make these interactions constructive and helpful, responding to the reasonable needs and concerns of the student while ensuring that appropriate standards are maintained. The presence of students on the postgraduate research committee helps to ensure feedback of general and specific student concerns. Progress reports at quarterly or bi-annual intervals also provide valuable insight.

Other measures may also be used to obtain such feedback in a less personalised and less confrontational way. Annual or even bi-annual postgraduate student workshops, organised to discuss general and particular student issues, are useful. Annual anonymous surveys of postgraduate students, using a questionnaire format, also allow students to provide valuable comments and suggestions.

It is essential that the rights of the postgraduate student be protected in this feedback process. Under no circumstances must the student be disadvantaged as a result of offering honest feedback. It may be most useful to gather such formal feedback from the student or graduate during the first year after they have left the institution. Then the feedback will tend to be well-balanced in that the graduate is much more autonomous and can be more objective than when still a registered student.

FURTHER PUBLICATIONS ON THE RESEARCH WORK

A key aim of postgraduate research work is the advancement and promulgation of knowledge. The publication of articles, books and other communications on the outcomes, implications and applications of the research is therefore an essential element of the work.

Each discipline has its own conventions and modes of publication. With the development of new electronic communication technologies, these conventions and modes are rapidly changing. Nevertheless at any time there tends to be a hierarchy of journals and conferences of different degrees of academic rigour and peer review and different audiences within the broad discipline and across the boundaries of the discipline. Acknowledged measures of the quality of the research are the conferences and journals in which it is published and the responses of the participants and readership to the work and its outcomes. It is at this stage that the greatest degree of peer review and recognition comes to bear on the work.

An alternative recognition of the worth of the research work is the commercial exploitation of the intellectual property developed in the work through patents, licences and industrial agreements and partnerships.

It is a vital aspect of quality assurance in respect of postgraduate research, that the institution maintains a record of the publications of all kinds arising from each such research project.

DEPARTMENTAL SELF-EVALUATION AT END OF RESEARCH PROJECT

After the project is completed and the student has left the institution, it is valuable for the department to review the project, not only in terms of the benefit to the student but also in terms of its outcomes for the department and institution. The head of department and the other staff members involved in supervision, as well as some other members of the department, should draw up a balance sheet of the project, its conduct, the difficulties encountered, the costs involved and the academic and other benefits to the department.

Such a self-study allows lessons to be learned for future work, these lessons to be communicated to a range of staff members and then priorities to be set for the on-going development of the postgraduate research effort in the department.

EVALUATION OF QUALITY IN RESEARCH

An activity as complex as research, which is highly dependent on physical resources, intellectual ability, co-operative interactions between different people and on the difficulty of the fundamental objectives of the work, does not readily yield to quantitative evaluation at an individual level. Nevertheless quality improvement and quality evaluation are recurring aspects of academic research in an increasing number of countries and has been attempted in recent years in Ireland on a pilot basis.[3]

A report on a "comparative international assessment of the organisation, management and funding of university research in Ireland and Europe" was prepared in 1996 by the consultants, the Circa Group, on behalf of the Higher Education Authority. Among the issues addressed were the accountability of the institutions in relation to research funding and the quality of the research done when benchmarked against international standards of bibliometric data and analysis of citations.

The report noted that formal external assessment of university research is carried out on a periodic basis in Britain, France, Sweden and Holland and in the Max Planck Institutes for basic science in Germany. Because of the globalisation of knowledge and, in particular, scientific knowledge, research in Ireland needs to strive for higher quality to be internationally competitive.

The methodology used by the Circa Group to broadly evaluate the research quality was the following bibliometric technique. The articles produced in each institution and published in a number of predetermined high quality refereed international journals were counted and analysed. The basic data on over 35,000 articles in total for the thirteen year period from 1981 to 1993 inclusive were obtained from the database of the Institute for Scientific Information (ISI) in Philadelphia. This organisation has maintained a multi-disciplinary scientific database on more than 4,000 key international scientific journals and over 3,000 social science and humanities journals for more than thirty years.[4]

---

[3] Higher Education Funding Councils, *Research Assessment Exercise* (London) 1994; Moed, H F and A M Ramaekers, *Bibliometric Profiles of Academic Biology Research in the Netherlands*, Report to the Association of Universities in the Netherlands (VSNU) (Leiden: Netherlands Quality Assessment of Research) 1994; Higher Education Authority, *A Comparative International Assessment of the Organisation, Management and Funding of University Research in Ireland and Europe,* Report of the CIRCA Group Europe (Dublin) 1996.

[4] Moed, H F and J G van der Velde, *Bibliometric Profiles of Academic Chemistry Research in the Netherlands*, Report to Netherlands Foundation for Chemical Research, Centre for Science and Technology, 1993; Winterhager, M, "Towards Bibliometric Object: a Relational View to ISI's Science Citation Index", in van Raan, A F et al., *Science and Technology in a Policy Context* (Leiden: DSWO Press) 1991.

The quality of these articles was then determined by using citation indicators. One such indicator was the number of times an article was subsequently cited in high quality publications. Furthermore this number was compared to the average or expected citation count for similar articles in comparable disciplines and sub-disciplines in comparable journals. Another indicator used was the extent of international collaboration involved in the work as evidenced by the number of international co-authors on the papers. Broadly, the higher these indicators are for an article the higher the perceived quality of the article relative to others in that specialism.

In the research assessment process in the universities in Britain, referred to in Chapter 3, the research effort is rated on a seven point comparative scale. This scale has the following seven qualitative grades of research quality:

5*   international level of excellence in most areas

5   international level in some areas and national level of excellence in most other areas

4   national level of excellence in most areas, close to international level in some

3a   national level of excellence in large majority of areas

3b   national level of excellence in most areas

2   national level of excellence in up to half of the areas

1   national level of excellence in almost no area.

The expert panel for the discipline makes comparative assessments as to whether the research profile of a department is of international level of excellence, of national level of excellence or of less than national level of excellence. Subsequently the assessments of all of the departments in an institution are compiled and an overall research quality grade computed for the institution as a whole. Attributing numerical marks to qualitative categories facilitates this latter stage. However, while comparison and averaging within a discipline may be justified, doing so across disciplines and between institutions can only be considered to be of dubious validity.

SUMMARY

In order to carry a postgraduate research project to a successful completion in an acceptable time, unique teamwork is required between postgraduate student and supervisor(s). However, wider peer review involving feedback from other researchers in the discipline and in related disciplines, within the institution and in other institutions, is also of key importance.

CHAPTER NINE

Guidelines for an Institutional Framework for Quality Assurance

Teaching, research and learning in higher education are carried out in the context of an academic institution, occasionally with the added involvement of an external research, business or industrial organisation. While the maintenance of standards and the assurance of quality in these activities, as they occur in classrooms, laboratories and libraries, rest heavily on the shoulders of academic staff, the supporting institutional framework — physical and human resources as well as social and cultural environment and ethos — has a vital role as well. The academic staff and students must be facilitated and supported in their work by an accessible and supportive institutional framework. There must be an appropriate physical and administrative structure, functioning in broad harmony with the standards of the academic activities and the mission of the institution. To ensure this harmony, feedback mechanisms must be in place to respond to and repair shortcomings observed by staff, students and other stakeholders.

All parties involved in the provision of education should act with professional integrity and in an ethical manner towards their students and also their colleagues and other institutional stakeholders. In a sense, the professional and ethical actions of staff encapsulate their commitment to quality and excellence. The institutional framework must be provided to underpin and give substance to this.

GOVERNANCE FRAMEWORK

In the governance of an institution, the commitment to quality must find clear expression in the charter, statutes, regulations and procedures, in the thoroughness and relevance of the strategic plan and in the professional functioning of the governing body and the academic and administrative management at all levels. Well-publicised and transparent management and committee structures, each with clear terms of reference, with each post and function thoroughly defined, with the lines of responsibility clearly mapped out and with defined ways of resolving conflicts, are fundamental requirements.

The commitment to quality is meaningful only if the resources are allocated in a transparent fashion and the staff as a whole are drawn positively into the ethos of quality and quality improvement through participation in the planning process and transparent communications throughout the institution. It is the responsibility of management to develop and foster in every way possible a pervasive respect for and drive towards excellence and continuing quality improvement.

The most immediate context in which the academic activities of a higher education institution are carried out is the department — the basic operational unit of the system. It is the most immediate part of the institutional framework underpinning the maintenance of standards, quality assurance and educational ethos. In its strategic planning, allocating of resources, staffing and ancillary servicing, the department must be equipped and managed in the spirit of quality enhancement and the achievement of excellence.

STRATEGIC PLANNING

Strategic planning is a widespread consultative and participative process in an institution and its component departments, designed to map out in detail its development path for the next three to five years. This process requires:

- a thorough and objective self-evaluation of the functioning of the institution, its faculties, departments and other sections over the previous number of years

- a clear statement of the constraints set by finance, accommodation, government policies, demography, social, economic, technological contexts at local, national and international levels, organisational inertia and impediments to change in the institution and the competitive environment nationally and internationally

- an expression of the academic, quality improvement and other organisational targets to be aimed for over the period of the plan.

Since in these processes an institution of higher education is highly dependent on public funding and subject to public regulation and accountability, relationships with the Department of Education and Science and other public bodies and representatives need particular attention in the process of strategic planning.

Such a thorough-going process, affecting every element of the institution, every member of staff, every function and every activity, requires the constructive involvement and partnership of the widest cross-section of the staff at all levels. But it must be organised in order to give it focus and to ensure an integrated and institutional structure to the overall strategic plan. Also the difficult process of setting and agreeing on the various priorities and of balancing between short term and medium term perspectives across the institution need to be co-ordinated carefully.

A vital aspect of strategic planning and the implementation of the strategic plan is change and its management. Change tends to emerge from a need for development or from some dissatisfaction with or external challenge to aspects of the current situation and can give rise to disquiet among staff. Implementing change requires assurance to staff that all are participants in the development and that representatives of the staff have a significant role to play in the process. Clarity, openness and trust are needed. Effective management and leadership involve empowering staff members at all levels so that they feel ownership of the changes and quality improvements envisaged.[1] In this respect, just as in the overall elaboration of the strategic plan, extensive consultation and communication are vital.

ACCOMMODATION AND RESOURCES

An institution must provide lecture, seminar and tutorial rooms, adequate in number, size and quality, equipped with modern teaching resources including video, computer and projection facilities, and safe and hygienic laboratories with a range of up-to-date equipment, which are suitable for their purpose and furnished with good-quality practical handbooks. The accommodation resources must broadly match the activities scheduled for their use in each department and discipline. The best-practice standards in these resources are changing rapidly and the accommodation available needs to be reviewed each year in the light of changing needs and emerging technologies.

A postgraduate research project can require extensive accommodation as well as equipment and other facilities. Indeed in some disciplines it may not be possible to foresee clearly the equipment and space requirements over the three to four year period of the work. Collaboration with other laboratories and institutions and occasional access to established facilities elsewhere may help to ensure adequate support for the project.

Feedback mechanisms must be provided for staff and students to comment and advise on the repair, maintenance and improvement of all facilities and, indeed, the general environment of the institution.

In order to facilitate and encourage self-directed learning among the student body, it is essential that considerable library and study resources and general common space be available for students to work, relax and socialise.

The prime common academic space for both students and staff is the library. It is the main scholarly nexus in an institution and the development

---

[1] Kouzes, J M and B Z Posner, *The Leadership Challenge* (San Francisco: Jossey-Bass Publishers) 2nd edition, 1995.

and resourcing of the library or libraries is a key litmus test of the commitment of the institution to quality enhancement and indeed to developing an ethos of learning and scholarship. While the library staff members provide a vital and on-going training service for students and academic staff, it is the responsibility of the academic staff to ensure, within budget constraints, the range and depth of the library holdings of books, journals and video and other electronic resources, are appropriate to serve the different disciplines.

With developments in methods of knowledge storage and retrieval through information and telecommunications technology, the nature of the library service is rapidly changing. Remote access is now possible and extensive information resources are available on the internet. This requires a physical computer network throughout the institution that is robust, well supported and maintained and regularly up-graded in the light of rapidly changing hardware and software technologies. It also requires a process of continual training and retraining of staff and students in the new technologies and their applications.

STAFF RECRUITMENT AND DEVELOPMENT

Without appropriate human resources, within an environment fostering good morale and a widely shared vision of and loyalty to the institution and its mission, the achievement of excellence can only be partial at best. The staff members at all grades and the broad partnership and teamwork between them are an educational institution's key resource and asset and their management is a key determinant of quality. Care for the staff and meaningful attention to supporting them, facilitating a partnership approach to all the work of the institution and providing for staff retraining and development needs, are fundamental tasks of the management of the institution.

Clearly these considerations apply to each department so that the institution as a whole is enabled to achieve excellence.

Academic staff are key players in the delivery of high quality academic programmes and in providing quality assurance and improvement. The academic capabilities of the staff should be matched to the teaching and training needs of the programmes offered by the institution. In order to ensure this matching, procedures must be in place to recruit the most appropriate staff according to defined criteria and guidelines, to induct and train them into the institution and its regulations, procedures and programmes, to provide career development guidance and support to each member of staff, to appraise the performance of each and facilitate helpful development and retraining opportunities to better match the staff to the changing functions of the institution.

Technical staff provide support for academic staff and students in workshop, studio and laboratory work and in relation to computing and communications activities. Library staff administer the library, maintaining book, journal and electronic stocks, inducting and training library users in new developments, helping to train students in library research methods and, in general, facilitating a scholarly atmosphere in the library. Administrators provide a wide range of personal services to students, staff and other stakeholders — public relations, registration and student records, assessments and related records, work and job placement and secretarial and other related support services for course committees (validation and review, regular administration, annual report) and course management. Porters and security staff present a public face of the institution to students, staff and other stakeholders. Maintenance staff work to ensure that all accommodation and the overall environment remain maximally functional, effective and safe.

All of these staff therefore play vital roles in the overall team, supporting the academic functions, providing services to students, staff and other stakeholders and generally creating a safe and caring environment in which teaching and learning can proceed with greatest effectiveness. In the case of all of these various categories of staff, appropriate recruitment criteria and procedures, as well as induction, development, encouragement and management processes, are as important as for academic staff.

The development of all of the staff members is a key step in developing quality and quality assurance in higher education. In order to effectively confront the competitive challenge of other world-class institutions, Dearing (1997) has pointed out that it is essential that there be investment in staff development and training and that this should continue throughout a teacher's academic career.[2] This same aim should apply to all members of staff of the institution.

A staff development programme can have among its goals the enhancement of the individual staff member's expertise in their discipline, in their teaching and the improvement of their morale and motivation. Staff development also relates to the functional and developmental needs of the institution, staffing levels, individual performance evaluation and matching staff skills and capabilities to the tasks required to deliver the mission. Clear information about the duties and responsibilities involved in performing each job and the skills and knowledge required to do it well, together with the help available, must be documented. On this foundation the training and development programme can be built.

Performance evaluation of staff may be used for promotional purposes, helping to determine development needs in different departments of the institution and identifying staff strengths and weaknesses, providing career planning advice and so helping to determine training programme priorities.

---

[2] Dearing, R, *Higher Education in the Learning Society*, Report of the National Committee of Inquiry into Higher Education (London) 1997.

In elaborating a staff development plan the management must address such issues as change management, performance enhancement, development of partnership and teamwork, human resource matters including forums in which all staff may express their concerns, industrial relations, political challenges and professional and ethical issues.

STUDENT NEEDS AND SERVICES

The higher education institution exists primarily to provide an educational service to students in a caring and friendly environment that fosters learning.

Service to students begins before their recruitment when information about the institution and its courses and programmes is provided to potential students. The quality and accuracy of this information should correspond to the general quality policies of the institution. The numbers recruited to each programme and their academic background and state of preparedness should be appropriate to that programme. Registration and issuance of student cards should be an efficient, well-organised and clearly defined process. It is of great benefit to both students and the institution itself that an induction process for new students be implemented. In this process, student handbooks and information packs on the institution, specific courses, resources and supports available, regulations for students including disciplinary criteria and procedures, information and guidance on issues of transition from second level to third level education, student representation on quality and other committees, mechanisms of student consultation, departmental and faculty student liaison officers or tutors, examination regulations and procedures and other valuable information can be communicated to the new students. It is also an opportunity for new students to meet staff and each other for the first time.

Good communication between the institution and its students in relation to such matters as class timetables and attendance, recording the submission of assigned work, schedules of assessments and examination schemes, publication of results and course and career guidance must continue throughout the course.

It is essential that views of students on the overall course, its content, organisation and presentation are obtained by such means as student survey questionnaire forms and staff/student meetings. Student feedback on matters such as their preparedness for the course, the balance and integration of the component subjects, the teaching methods, the organisation of lectures and tutorials, the quality and production of handouts and visual aids, physical state of lecture and tutorial rooms, library facilities, laboratories, equipment, IT facilities, general environment of the institution and health and safety issues should be systematically compiled. In addition student feedback on assessment procedures and standards, effectiveness of communications, course administration, staff responsiveness to student comments, questions and suggestions and level of academic leadership provided, provides a key input to the annual course monitoring report.

Student membership of the course committees, at least one student representative for each year of the course, allows more immediate feedback to prevent problems developing and to deal more effectively with problems that arise.

Staff/student meetings, held at least twice each academic year and organised by the course committee, are another means of obtaining student feedback and can lead to early adjustment and improvement in course delivery or other aspects that are of concern.

The accumulation of student feedback, by surveys and by staff/student meetings and other methods, over a number of years of operating a course, help to inform the critical self-study and provide a valuable input into the periodic course review. Responsiveness to student feedback is a key element of the quality enhancement process.

The students' representative organisation or students' union generally represents the interests of students in the institution and promotes the social and organisational side of student life, including the clubs and societies. It helps to provide a comprehensive support service to students and brings general student concerns to the attention of management at the appropriate level. It also provides general information, and financial and welfare advice. In this regard, it is necessary that the officers of the union work closely with the student services office of the institution and with the counsellors and chaplains.

CULTURAL, SOCIAL AND WELFARE ENVIRONMENT

The institution's student accommodation service should provide advice and guidance to students in finding living accommodation, whether through institutional student housing or the inspection and accreditation of private accommodation within reasonable travelling distance of the institution.

Information should also be made available to students about the services and facilities available in the city and region in which the institution is located, such as social, cultural, sporting, recreational and transport facilities.

Overseas students need special attention in terms of their induction, integration and guidance. The institution should provide a special handbook for this purpose giving contact names and taking account of the cultural differences and challenges facing such students.

Facilities should be provided to students, such as access to appropriate common spaces and rooms, for social, sporting and cultural events. They should also be provided with reasonable finances and support to organise and run clubs and societies to cover all of the major and minor sporting disciplines, as well as cultural and social activities and, indeed, various course- and discipline-related professions. Sports officers and coaches should be funded by the institution to facilitate these clubs. Institutional sports teams can contribute considerably to the morale and spirit within the institution and should be organised where possible. These clubs and societies should be open for membership to full-time and part-time students from across the institution.

The institution should attach high priority to enhancing the services it provides for its students at all levels. Young students in particular need considerable support at the most formative stage of their lives and careers and the institution should provide this in so far as is possible with available resources.

A student health service, supplemented by dispersed first aid services and access to a hospital accident and emergency service, should also be provided. Obviously a personal accident insurance scheme should also be in place in the institution, with a wide range of benefits in respect of certified accidents that occur, irrespective of whether a student or staff member is on institution premises or elsewhere.

A confidential counselling service for students, staffed by a team of professional counselling psychologists, should also be provided to help students identify and resolve difficulties that may impinge on their academic and personal development. Such a service may also offer a variety of valuable training programmes on topics such as time management, study and communication skills, stress management and assertiveness, for example.

A team of chaplains representative of different religions and faiths should be made available for pastoral care and can be complementary to the counselling service.

In order to assist students with special needs, the institution should also provide areas of social welfare support to supplement the support publicly available. A service should also be provided to help students with disabilities such as physical disability, dyslexia and others.

An appointments and careers service should also be provided to help students and recent graduates obtain employment. This service should offer advice on the job market, job application skills, teamwork, interview techniques and career opportunities.

COMMUNICATIONS

The achievement of quality in all of the activities and functions of a higher education institution requires the maximum clarity of communication and transparency of procedures. The mission, constitution or charter, statutes and regulations must be published and made available to staff, students and other stakeholders. Handbooks and information packs, particularly designed for different disciplines, should be prepared and disseminated. All of this information should also be made available on the institution's web site.

Changes and developments should be reported in newsletters and on the web site. Workshops or seminars should be organised in the departments, faculties and other units to discuss, explain, correct and further disseminate these materials.

ACADEMIC AND RESEARCH ETHOS

The ethos of a higher education institution is developed and shaped principally by the professionalism of the staff at all levels. The scholarship of the members of academic staff, their research activities, the product or service development and consultancy services they provide to external stakeholders, their publications and research grants, the seminars they present on their work, the outcomes of their research and its impact on the courses they teach, the industrial, business and other applications of their findings, the publicity achieved for academic achievements in teaching, research and scholarship, the facilitation of feedback from students to staff and management, the ethos of improvement in academic and administrative matters, all of these and others help to generate and keep vibrant a dynamic and scholarly ethos in the institution.

It is the responsibility of the management to positively underpin, facilitate and give recognition to all of the multi-faceted and inter-linked contributions made by different members of staff to forming and maintaining this ethos.

Intellectual property may arise in the course of research work in the institution. Where such intellectual property is exploited to create employment or improve a product or service for society, it can add to the scholarly reputation and morale of the institution.

The institution should have an ethics committee with a remit to develop a code of research and teaching ethics and monitor the compliance of all research and teaching carried out under the aegis of the institution with that code.

EXTERNAL LINKS

The multiplicity of links which the institution and its departments and individual staff members have with external higher education institutions within the country and abroad provide many levels of benchmarking and comparison between its own activities and those of other leading institutions. Monitoring of the examination process by external examiners is a definitive assessment of the quality of an academic programme. External representation on validation and review panels helps to provide further assurance about standards reached. Relationships with professional bodies that accredit courses for membership purposes also provide strong elements of quality assurance. When members of staff of the institution serve as external experts for other institutions, reassuring benchmarking can also occur. Links with industry and commerce and other outside experts in research and development, in consultancy and in the design or review of courses, help to confirm quality assurance and improvement. External academic visitors who spend some time and deliver lectures and seminars within the institution help to develop and confirm the institution's standards of quality. Participation in national and international research collaborations with prestigious universities and other research and industrial organisations can be a powerful factor in developing the reputation of the institution, not only for the highest academic contributions, but also for its flexibility and responsiveness to the needs of society at home and abroad.

EQUITY OF ACCESS TO HIGHER EDUCATION

Clearly the quality achieved by an institution is presented particularly to its students — to those students who achieve places on its courses. However, it is well established that there are many candidates for these places who, through economic, social, physical, language, gender and other factors, do not achieve a place.[3] The demands of quality and social equity require that the institution adopt policies to achieve equity of access for the disadvantaged and implement them meaningfully across its academic provision.

In the Republic of Ireland places on full time higher education courses are allocated on the relatively objective basis of points scored in the Irish leaving certificate examination and the social origins or any other aspects of students are not taken directly into account. Nevertheless the participation rates in higher education, for instance, from large sections of the city of Dublin, are much lower than the national average. In order to combat this social exclusion a range of possible remedies including alternative mechanisms of entry, scholarships, special tutoring for students in certain second level schools and others should be developed. A major investment in such remedies is necessary to make a substantial impact.

---

[3] Clancy, P, *Access to College: Patterns of Continuity and Change* (Dublin: Higher Education Authority) 1995.

SAFETY, WELFARE AND INSURANCE COVER

The institution must maintain adequate insurance cover for its activities (employer's, product, professional, third party, public liability, etc.) to ensure that parties injured by the institution or its staff as they carry out their normal duties may be indemnified, while the financial and physical integrity of the institution itself is also protected.

> An employer is jointly and severally liable for any tort (wrongful act, injury or damage — not involving a breach of contract —for which a civil action can be brought) committed by an employee while acting in the course of his employment. This may apply even though the act of the employee is not for the employer's benefit and even though he has expressly prohibited it. . . . This (vicarious liability) is sometimes difficult to prove but any party making a claim is usually influenced by the fact that the employer is more likely to be able to satisfy the claim by injured persons . . . .[4]

Research work involving external bodies can give rise to considerable risk of tort. It is essential that insurance cover for such work be obtained before the work begins and that the sharing of the cost of the insurance cover between the institution and the external body be included in the agreement or contract agreed for the work.

SUMMARY

The general quality assurance and enhancement procedures within an institution characterise the academic and scholarly ethos of that institution. Such an institution is caring in relation to its staff, students and society. It is professionally and transparently managed and administered throughout, is thorough, intelligent and widely consultative in its planning and is accountable academically, financially and socially to its students and to the wider society.

---

[4] AVEC, *Research and Consultancy in the VEC Colleges* (Dublin) 1982.

CHAPTER TEN

Principles of the Departmental, Faculty and Institutional Audit

An institutional quality audit is a review of the overall institution in respect of its quality assurance systems. The principles of a quality audit of an institution are broadly the same as those underpinning a quality audit of a sub-unit of the overall institution such as a faculty or department, except for scale and context.

NATURE OF THE QUALITY AUDIT

The aim of a quality review or audit is to evaluate the academic structures, procedures and standards of the institution, faculty or department in order to satisfy customers of the institution, other stakeholders and the funding authorities that the educational awards of the institution are of the quality claimed.[1]

The audit is organised by an agency external to and independent of the institution and is implemented by an audit panel appointed by the agency.[2] Normally such a panel comprises experienced academic and industrial members who are knowledgeable about higher education and academic quality assurance arrangements in Ireland and abroad. Secretarial support to the audit panel should be provided by the agency.

The audit agency sets the conditions and criteria for the audit and the audit panel evaluates the quality assurance procedures for the institution, faculty or department, seeking to ensure that they are:

• consistent with the institution's aims and objectives

• robust, rigorous and effective

• self-renewing and subject to continuous review and enhancement

---

[1] Higher Education Quality Council, *Learning from Audit 2* (London) 1996.
[2] Higher Education Quality Council, *Notes for the Guidance of Auditors* (London) 1995.

- such as to facilitate quality improvement
- supported by students and staff
- inclusive of external peer review
- such as to ensure that outcomes of the process lead to the establishment of standards which are recognised nationally and internationally and are acceptable to students, employers and professional bodies.

The audit panel first meets to decide on the outline and timetable for the required process. Normally the process requires a documented critical self-evaluation by the institution or sub-unit of the institution itself of its quality assurance procedures, to be submitted by a due date. The audit panel then reviews this documentation, and plans and conducts an extended visit to the institution. Finally the panel drafts its report on the audit. The institution is given the opportunity to review and comment on the draft report before the final report is submitted to the audit agency. The format in which the final report is published depends on the statutory arrangements and responsibilities of the audit agency. Preferably such reports should be in the public domain to inform the government, students, parents, industrialists and the general public.

THE QUALITY ASSURANCE AUDIT

The critical self-evaluation report of the quality assessment procedures within the institution or its sub-unit should be concise and comprehensive, giving descriptive and evaluative information and highlighting weaknesses as well as strengths. The self-evaluation documentation is normally to be placed in the context of the institution's mission. The documentation should therefore address the questions of what the institution is trying to do, how it does it and how well do its procedures work.

Specifically the institution's self-evaluation report should have the following elements:

- outline of the institution
- management and organisational structure
- academic profile
- quality assurance policies, structures and procedures in relation to course planning, design, teaching, learning, assessment and related staff and student issues
- quality assurance policies and procedures in relation to postgraduate research and other research and consulting work done by the staff of the institution

- quality assurance measures in relation to the management and administration of the institution's resources
- financial position
- data on staff
- data on students
- outline of the institution's facilities
- external relationships
- overall institutional self-evaluation
- an account of the institution's capacity for change.

The self-evaluation report should rest as much as possible on the standard publications of the institution such as prospectuses, handbooks and annual reports.

In order to formulate and present a thorough self-evaluation report on the institution as a whole, it is advisable that a working group should be formed to manage, drive and document the internal self-evaluation. The academic council should endorse and provide full support for the process. Individual self-evaluations for each department of the institution should be organised at the early stages of the process and in line with the audit outline specifications. It is essential that all members of staff be constructively facilitated to participate in this process and that the maximum amount of support be allocated to the process to ensure its success.

In order to develop staff involvement in the process, the chief officer of the institution should visit every department to explain the process and assure all staff of the commitment of the top management to the audit. The members of the working group should participate in information meetings throughout the institution, including meetings with administrative staff and student representatives. The use of external facilitators may be of value in these meetings.

The issues arising in the self-evaluation and the draft material for the self-evaluation report should be priority items on the agenda of the regular academic council meetings. It may be necessary to hold a number of special meetings of the council during the period of the self-evaluation to deal with issues that arise.

The staff should be regularly informed of the progress of the self-evaluation and the issues arising. A regular audit newsletter, circulated to all staff of the institution and made available on the institution's web site, may facilitate this process. It can help to clarify the outline requirements, solicit suggestions, provide information about the progress of the process and any problems encountered and remind staff of deadlines and other matters. Regular information and discussion meetings in the departments can also help in the process.

The self-evaluation process consists of a thorough internal questioning and analysis of the activities of the institution at as fundamental a level as possible. Core educational issues as well as those of institutional structure, identity and values should be debated widely across the institution. A possible, but not exhaustive, list of issues that might be discussed includes:

- the integration of the academic process of course design, development, assessment, examination, quality assurance

- the role of external examiners and other mechanisms of peer review

- the development and improvement of the mechanisms of student feedback

- the process of academic planning in the institution

- how comprehensively are the processes of course review, new course proposal and course validation, carried out according to the quality assurance procedures and improvements needed in these procedures

- the processes of developing an academic strategic plan for the institution as a whole, for each department and faculty, for the institution's library and information technology and communications services

- the development of postgraduate research in each department and faculty

- the management of issues relating to postgraduate taught courses

- research and consultancy for industry in the institution

- co-operation agreements with academic institutions and corporate organisations (for research, staff exchange, student exchange, sharing of facilities, sharing of courses)

- the structure of courses in the context of the proposed national qualifications framework

- the planning for course modularisation and credit accumulation

- clarifying the roles and responsibilities of members of the academic council and of committees of that council, emphasising their representative and information/decision communication roles

- reviewing the staff development programme and its management

- staff resources, accommodation (academic, administrative and social) and facilities

- reviewing the communications pathways and the responsibility/organisation trees throughout the institution

- improving the scholarly ethos and academic environment of the institution

- reviewing all prospectuses and planning of other publicity documentation, such as institutional profile, reports on research, videos, posters, music, exhibitions and others

- student facilities, social, sporting, academic, health and welfare.

Following individual department meetings, and in order to prepare a documented academic profile of each department, meetings of heads and assistant heads of department, moderated by members of the working group are necessary. In these meetings, it is useful to carry out a strengths/weaknesses/opportunities/threats (SWOT) analysis of each department. In this process the following listings and details may be documented about each department:

- good features or strengths of the department and how they might be developed and promoted

- weak features of the department and practical ways of addressing them

- other problems and impediments to progress and practical ways in which they might be addressed

- relevant needs of industry or society not being addressed rapidly and flexibly by the department, indicating priority actions to be taken in this regard

- the impact of quality assurance on the department and how it can be improved

- strengths and weaknesses of the quality assurance procedures as they affect the department

- developments in the department which would be desirable, in one to three years, four to seven years and eight to ten years

- new courses, according to the priority of the department, which should be developed, with a rationale for each and an outline of the additional resources of staff, accommodation, equipment and budget, required over the next five years

- courses in the department which should be phased out, with a rationale for each and an outline of the resource savings by these measures

- measures needed to improve the teaching, learning and assessment environment in the institution, in terms of class and lecture rooms, staff training, use of technology, role of library, course modularisation, research facilities, staff rooms and facilities and any other features

- appropriate balance for the department of postgraduate work (research and courses), primary degree and diploma and certificate work, apprenticeship courses and short courses in terms of staff work and student numbers

- main advantages and disadvantages of research, development and consultancy in the department, in the context of the mission of the institution

- priority five-year targets relative to research, development and consultancy in the department
- strengths and weaknesses of the management and organisational structure of the department in the overall context of the institution
- measures needed to achieve change for the better in the department
- ways in which the department, faculty and institution as a whole should promote itself in industry and society.

With regard to each department, comprehensive details should be compiled for each member of academic staff, for the previous three to five academic years. The following information is relevant:

- name and staff number
- academic qualifications (awarding institution and year) and professional memberships (professional body, membership grade and year of accession to this grade)
- current staff grade with year of appointment
- previous staff grades with years of appointment, if relevant
- nature of current appointment (full time, part time, contract or other)
- specialist teaching areas (level of courses taught and extent of responsibility)
- teaching experience in the institution (courses, years, subjects taught and periods of these responsibilities)
- specialist research areas (details of projects, numbers of postgraduate students, research grants and other relevant details)
- current research involvement (period, project titles, sponsors, results and outcomes)
- current development and consultancy involvement
- administrative and committee membership within the institution and other service to the institution
- work experience before appointment to the institution (period, employers, positions held and outline of responsibilities)
- involvement in professional bodies (officerships, committees)
- courses, seminars and workshops attended over past five years (date, title of course and location)
- conferences attended over past five years (date, title and location)

- publications, exhibitions and performances over past five years (date, title, location and reference)

- special achievements, prizes or awards (date, title and details)

- record of review or evaluation of performance with head of department, comments of head of department and those of staff member.

In respect of each course in the institution (master's degree, postgraduate diploma, primary degree, diploma, certificate, full-time and part-time), the relevant course committee should compile the following information:

- composition of the course committee

- annual course reports for the previous three academic years

- total numbers of students, broken down into male and female, full-time or part-time, and mature students

- numbers of first and overall preferences on the Central Applications Office (CAO) system for the past three years

- spread of leaving certificate points and any other significant details about student attainment levels at entry over the past three years

- enrolment trends

- completion rates, including numbers and percentages completing in normal time and in one, two and three years extra

- average teaching hours per student rating for each year and for the course as a whole

- senior, junior and part-time academic staff allocation to the course

- student contact hours, an estimate of student study load and ECTS credit allocations

- numbers of graduates and percentages achieving each grade of award

- employment statistics for graduates.

In relation to postgraduate research work in the department, the following information should be compiled:

- numbers of postgraduate research students in each of the postgraduate registers, each year for the past five years

- numbers of vacancies for postgraduate research students

- numbers of graduates with postgraduate diploma (research), master's degree by research and doctoral degree, each year for past five years

- numbers of staff members active in research supervision

- numbers of staff members experienced in successfully supervising postgraduate students to graduation at each level of postgraduate research award

- numbers of advisory or mentoring supervisors at each level of postgraduate award

- numbers of research grants each year for the past five years and awarding bodies

- cumulative amounts of research grants each year for past five years

- numbers of refereed publications, each year for past five years, with references

- numbers and references of other publications, exhibitions and scholarly outputs, each year for past five years.

The quality assurance committees should prepare reports on the implementation of the institution's quality assurance procedures for the courses and other activities within their remit.

Course annual reports prepared by the course committee should be compiled for each of the past three to five academic years, together with resulting actions and comments by the relevant quality assurance committee.

The reports on any course reviews and validations over the previous three to five years should also be compiled. These contain observations and recommendations, with strong elements of external peer review, on the courses involved.

The documentation prepared for the audit panel may fall into four categories — the main self-evaluation report; accompanying documentation to underpin and illustrate the self-evaluation report; appendices, giving factual information to amplify some aspects of the self-evaluation report and provide statistical information on students and staff and background supporting documentation, including prospectuses, pertinent reports and other appropriate material produced by the institution.

The critical self-evaluation report might include sections covering the following aspects:

- brief outline of the institution — formal mission, aims and goals

- management and organisational structure of the institution — organisational arrangements and oversight of academic affairs, decision-making process and role and function of senior officers and committees, budget mechanism and its transparency, co-ordination between departments and central administration and mechanisms for resolving conflicts

- academic profile of the institution — list of courses and programmes (including externally accredited courses), academic development plan, proposed new courses, undergraduate and postgraduate, expected year of introduction and rationale, arrangements for student transfer between courses (internally and externally), areas of research strength, strategy for development of research, responsiveness to local, regional, national and international needs, structure of programmes, e.g. modularisation, etc.

- institution's quality assurance policies, structures and procedures — course planning and design, market testing, evidence of demand or need for new programmes, curriculum design, content, innovation, organisation, internal course approval procedures, external validation procedures, management and allocation of staff resources, assessment of relevance and effectiveness (views of students, employers, external examiners, how are these co-ordinated, follow-up action, etc.), review procedures, strategy for teaching, learning, assessment policies, implementation and evaluation, student progress and achievement

- staff issues — staff training and development in research, teaching and assessment, policies in relation to management of human resources, quantitative data with comments, staff recruitment policies and procedures, terms and conditions of employment of academic staff, appraisal and advancement and reward criteria, equity and equality of opportunity and staff development

- student issues — support systems for students, student appeals system, involvement of students in evaluation procedures, quantitative data with comments, access and admissions procedures, progression and achievements

- financial position of the institution — budget and outturn for the previous years and estimated expenditure for the current year, sources of funding, breakdown of expenditure by categories (academic departments, library, premises, etc.), financial management, autonomy and delegation of resources

- accommodation and facilities — buildings, laboratories, in relation to staff and student numbers, locations, age, details of academic support facilities such as the library (book stock, places per student, etc.), computer resources and access and social and sports facilities

- external relationships — liaison and co-operation with other academic institutions, industry, commerce, public agencies, professional bodies, student and staff mobility and international links

- overall institutional self-evaluation — relative maturity of departments and faculties in academic development and achievement and the awards offered and the institution's capacity for change as demonstrated by its responsiveness to internal and external demands, needs and opportunities.

The key accompanying documentation should include the following:

- quality assurance procedures
- examination regulations and procedures
- enabling legislation.

The appendices provided should include the following:

- historical profile of the institution
- tables and details of industrial and international links
- outline of the historical development of quality assurance procedures in the institution
- tables of student data
- tables of staff data.

Background supporting documents, mostly institutional documentation, should be made available to the audit panel. They would include the following:

- prospectuses
- student handbooks
- reviews of research and development projects in the institution
- reports on previous reviews or audits of the institution or its sub-units
- policy documents on equality of opportunity in employment, preventing sexual harassment, safety, health and welfare at work, disability and access for the disadvantaged, etc.

The draft self-evaluation report should be discussed and approved by the academic council before submission to the audit panel. After submission and before the institutional visit by the audit panel, this self-evaluation report should be further presented by the working party and discussed in each of the main academic forums in the institution — academic council, each committee of the academic council, faculty boards, senior administrators and student representatives.

THE INSTITUTIONAL VISIT BY THE AUDIT PANEL

The audit panel should spend a number of days in the institution, depending on its size and scope, discussing the self-evaluation report in detail with the management and senior staff and, in particular, the academic council and its committees, the working group, and other groups including staff, students, graduates, some course committees and others that it may wish to meet. The panel should also tour the facilities in general. On the final day of the visit, the audit panel should hold a general review and summary meeting with the senior management team of the institution to resolve any remaining issues, before meeting privately to draft its report.

REPORT OF THE AUDIT PANEL

The first major part of the report of the audit panel should be its assessment of the institution in the light of the self-evaluation report, its visit to the institution, its meetings with staff at the different levels and students and graduates. This assessment should be according to the criteria set out for the audit.

The report to the audit agency should also contain recommendations concerning the institution and its programmes. These recommendations may relate to the balance of programmes offered by the institution, to weaknesses that need to be strengthened, or possibly to the suitability of the criteria set for the audit. In the case of an institution regularly failing to reach generally acceptable standards, there would exist the possibility of recommendations to terminate accreditation for certain programmes and activities.

The audit panel also should make a number of recommendations to the institution and provide advice on how to strengthen weaknesses observed, improve programmes and procedures, avail of opportunities and avoid pitfalls. Generally such recommendations should be given in a constructive and helpful manner to enable the institution to enhance its provision and reach standards comparable to national and international benchmarks.

Finally the report should include the comments of the institution on the draft report and in particular its responses to the recommendations and its plans in relation to them.

IMPLEMENTATION OF THE RECOMMENDATIONS IN THE AUDIT PANEL REPORT

It is of the greatest importance that the institution implement the recommendations of the audit panel report, to the extent possible and with all possible urgency, within budgetary and other physical constraints. Certainly, within a culture of periodic quality audits, each such audit after the first one is very likely to begin with a review of the outcome and aftermath of the previous one.

In this way the institutional quality audit will, over time, become a key instrument of benchmarking and quality enhancement in relation to the academic provision of the institution as a whole.

The process of preparing for and undergoing the quality audit can be a cathartic and revitalising experience for the institution, in that its staff has to comprehensively and critically review old assumptions and practices and, as a community, reassert its mission and direction. It can equally be an uncomfortable experience, raising the need for change and renewal and revealing not only strengths but also weaknesses. It can raise a wide range of academic, management and even personal issues at all levels in the institution. Not all such issues can be resolved in the self-evaluation process itself, but their resolution in the medium term can help to shape and revitalise the orientation and activities of the institution in the following years.

SUMMARY

The quality audit of a department, faculty or institution as a whole is a formal evaluation of the unit and of the academic and administrative functioning of that unit by authoritative external peers. It provides a key oversight of the unit and a calibration of the internal self-study evaluation. It is an objective and independent benchmarking of the unit or institution and provides a set of helpful and constructive recommendations for quality enhancement.

CHAPTER ELEVEN

Quality Assurance Developments in the Next Decade

Higher education institutions in Ireland would claim that they have always striven for quality and excellence in their activities and always fostered an ethos of improvement as part of their mission. However, they have not been able to offer, and do not yet offer, objective assurance in relation to quality to any appreciable degree.

In the past, the institutions did not feel the need to explicitly declare their missions. Until recently they would have felt no need for a statement of their mission or for a strategic plan of action for a period into the future. Serious comparisons with leading "benchmark" institutions elsewhere in the world would not have been made.

But the revolutionary change, from elite institutions with small classes and more or less socially coherent student groups with relatively narrow ranges of ability to mass education institutions with large classes and wide social diversity and wide range of ability, is now well underway in Ireland. The need to manage this change is pressing. Moreoever the notion of service to students and society is becoming more demanding than ever before. The concept of a multi-faceted, holistic and caring learning institution is gaining ground as the organisational paradigm of the higher education institution in this new age.

Technological change, international competition and the increasing need in the marketplace for national and international equivalence of degrees, diplomas and certificates provide powerful motivation for quality assurance in the higher education institutions. The related need for improved student and graduate mobility and the inexorably developing international co-operation in higher education teaching, research and scholarly activities in general all impel the higher education institutions in the same direction.

Most significantly, the government paymaster is driving these changes in the activities of the higher education institutions.

There is underway, therefore, a fundamental redrafting of the social contract between society and the higher education institutions in Ireland and internationally.

The concepts and procedures of institutional quality assurance and improvement are key to these changes. The implementation of procedures of quality assurance, along the lines described in this book, across the higher education institutions in Ireland is unavoidable, necessary and, "if taken in the flood", can be of great benefit to students and the institutions themselves.

WHO DETERMINES AND ASSURES QUALITY?

Many aspects of quality, quality assurance and quality enhancement in higher education institutions remain unclear. What should the extent and nature of the quality assurance be in these institutions? What is the most appropriate approach to implementing these procedures? What philosophy should drive the internal and relatively subjective processes of quality assurance within each institution? What authority should drive the external and more objective auditing processes involving peer review on behalf of students, society, government and other stakeholders?

There are many possible impediments to developing a quality system in the higher education institutions in Ireland. Some of these impediments have been indicated or implied in earlier chapters.

Many academics in higher education believe that their institutions and their specific disciplines have an intellectual and professional cohesion and efficiency that need not be answerable to government or to public opinion. They contend that teaching can not be quantitatively assessed or evaluated and assigned performance indices according to any meaningful efficiency criteria. They question how research work can be evaluated on a quantitative scale and compared to the quantitative scales for teaching and academic activities such as administration, student and public interaction and others. Academics acknowledge that if evaluations of these diverse activities are to be used to determine funding, they will be likely to readjust their activities to maximise funding, but possibly without improving the service to students and society and possibly distorting disciplines, departments and faculties.

The allegation has been made that the imposition of quality assurance systems by institutions of government represents a serious government mistrust of the professionalism and integrity of academic staff. It is argued that this mistrust poses a threat to staff morale, which in turn could cause a degradation of the quality of academic activities and results. It is certainly essential that any quality assurance mechanisms must support and encourage the inner drive, motivation and integrity of teachers and researchers which make them inspiring and their work excellent.

Quality assurance might be viewed as calling into question many aspects of the nature of the teaching process and the teaching profession. Certainly the situation, fairly unique to higher education, in which the individual teacher is the principal assessor of the efficacy of their personal work, is called into question by the requirements of quality assurance. It is difficult to cogently argue for this situation to continue in a democratic society. External (both national and international) and internal peer review of examination processes, the main conventional overview and benchmarking of higher education teachers for generations, is limited in time and depth and provides little insight into the day-to-day and month-to-month teaching effectiveness of a teacher or of a course team or department. How long does an initial qualification achieved through higher education retain its validity and vitality and how much and how often must each teacher be retrained and updated to retain currency? How should the quality of this updating of knowledge and skill be assured? How well does any higher education course or programme prepare the graduate for a career characterised more and more by lifelong learning?

Most higher level teaching is a team activity *par excellence.* Many component subjects and many subject elements taught by many individual teachers constitute the course experienced by the student. Quality assurance procedures help to optimise the partnership and teamwork needed to give coherence to the service received by the students. For this reason, it would be highly counter-productive if teachers sought to opt out of quality assurance and quality improvement activities. It is vital therefore that all necessary measures be taken to facilitate and encourage the highest level of enthusiastic participation by all staff in these procedures.

Quality assurance procedures should be shaped and implemented through full consultation and discussion with the participants, in order to overcome the inherent inertia of large institutions. The processes must also take account of the much valued diversity of different institutions, each with long-developed traditions, and local and other particular structures. It is highly desirable that quality assurance systems be integrated into the normal academic activities and allocated necessary additional resources. It is vital that the system minimises bureaucratic requirements that would alienate the staff involved and waste time that could be more effectively spent.

There are questions regarding the ability of any external body to objectively evaluate the quality of so complex an organisation as a higher education institution, engaged in carrying out so complex a process as teaching and learning. Such evaluation is limited in time and carried out on the basis of relatively limited observation and evidence. Yet only such an evaluation can provide some element of objective comparison between and calibration of institutions. Certainly the individual higher education institution can not provide such objective evaluation.

Concern has been expressed as to what use will be made of quality evaluations and quality audit results. Who will adjudge that self-improvement achieved in programmes or performance indicators or numerical quality measures is adequate? Will there be public league tables of individual staff members based on their teaching, research and administrative excellence, or league tables of departments and institutions? Will there be linkage between effectiveness of the quality assurance and improvement procedures and government funding? What form might this linkage take? If poor quality persists over time in an institution or a department of an institution, how will the cause be diagnosed and what actions will be taken to ensure improvement? If poor comparative quality persists in an institution or a department, will the funding agencies, and indeed will market forces, allow this to continue for long?

It is clear that significant industrial relations issues arise in relation to quality assurance. There is need for an extensive consultative process to persuade academics of the value of such systems and procedures. Like many circumstances of ferment and controversy, quality assurance processes do offer challenges but also opportunities to academics to develop and guarantee their effectiveness and that of their institution before the critical eyes of public opinion. In that quality assurance procedures would appear to foreshadow elements of the future development and shape of the higher education teaching profession, it would be highly desirable and even advisable for the academics to embrace quality assurance and thereby take the initiative themselves in actively reshaping and reforming their profession.

QUALITY ASSURANCE AND AN ETHOS OF ACADEMIC EXCELLENCE

An important aspect of academic quality assurance and quality improvement is not only improved courses and research and higher calibre graduates, but also the development of an institutional culture and ethos of excellence. Such a culture tends to foster positive attitudes to standards of excellence in all aspects of the institution's activities. According to Oakland, quality assurance "controls and techniques are important, but they are not the primary requirement. It is more an attitude of mind based on a pride in the job, and requiring total commitment from the top, which must be then extended to all employees at all levels".[1]

Quality in education includes the notions of excellence and value indicating that quality has both a utilitarian and an intellectual and creative dimension. These two dimensions are connected with what van Vught called the "internal" and "external" considerations of quality measurement.[2]

On the one hand, the academic community sees excellence in higher education as being associated with processes inherent in the development and integration of knowledge and with intelligence, competence and creativity. This internal aspect of quality is exemplified by the model of the self-governing community of scholars who overview and evaluate each other's contributions

---

[1] Oakland, J S, *Total Quality Management* (Oxford: Heinemann Professional) 1989.
[2] van Vught, F A, "Intrinsic and Extrinsic Aspects of Quality Assessment in Higher Education" in Westerheijden, D F et al. (eds), *Changing Contexts of Quality Assessment* (Utrecht: LEMMA) 1994.

to the body of knowledge and the scientific and general community. In this model, sometimes referred to as the English model, decisions about quality in education are taken by academic colleagues through peer review.

The external aspect, the value of higher education to society in general, comes to the fore in what is referred to as the French model, based on "the French practice of vesting control in an external authority".[3] This model epitomises the more recent movement towards accountability in educational quality, outlined in this book. The power to decide what may be identified as quality in education in this model is largely in the hands of an external authority. The academics are accountable to the external authority for the content and quality of their teaching and research.

An educational institution must relate its performance to its mission. A better performing institution pursues higher standards of service in support of its mission. Leaders of such an institution continuously search for ways to create and sustain a committed team of educators that will identify actively with the purpose of their institution as, for instance, a high reputation for research in a particular field, a superior tutorial system or excellence in teaching in its specific disciplines. Quality assurance procedures provide an indispensable tool in this endeavour.

THE CHANGING ROLE OF HIGHER EDUCATION IN SOCIETY — TOWARDS MASS HIGHER EDUCATION

Barnett described how the relationships between higher education, knowledge and society are changing profoundly.[4] Higher education has become pivotal in society, having grown enormously in size in recent times. The university has lost its monopoly over the definitions and production of knowledge. Also, in modern society literacy is not the universal problem it once was and the population as a whole is more informed.

With the drive throughout much of the world to increase access to and participation in higher education, the nature and role of higher education and the higher education institutions are changed forever. The new mass character of higher education implies fundamental changes in the teaching and learning processes in these institutions. The growth in applied knowledge and in the forms and availability of that knowledge also impinge deeply on these processes. The emphasis on lifelong learning, the constant, urgent need for upskilling and retraining, not only of staff in industry and business but also of academic and other staff in the higher education institutions themselves,

---

[3] Cobban, A B, *The Medieval English University, Oxford and Cambridge to c. 1500* (Berkeley: University of California Press) 1988, p. 124.

[4] Barnett, R, "Beyond Competence", in Coffield, F and W Williamson, *Repositioning Higher Education* (Buckingham: Open University Press) 1997.

present unprecedented challenges and opportunities to these institutions. The opportunities are presented for the higher education institutions to make much greater contribution than ever before to improving the human condition in general and to enhancing intellectual life.

With the growing centrality and scope of higher education in society and the increasing financial input by government to the institutions, issues of accountability and value for money to society and the state have become very significant. These are not simple concepts in relation to higher education. For instance, the institution's accountability to its students can be quite different from its accountability to the government paymaster. In trying to determine measures of value for money or efficiency, how can the inputs and outputs of so complex a system — the so-called added value — be objectively measured?

Autonomy or academic freedom has long been a watchword of the universities and other higher education institutions. This has generally been taken to denote the right of individual teachers to pursue their own lines of study within the standards of their disciplines, coupled with the right of the university itself to establish its internal structures and priorities and organise its external links and relationships. Clearly the academic freedom of the university has never been absolute but, rather, conditional and limited by its contract with society and the government, mediated in Ireland since 1968 by the Higher Education Authority (HEA).

The requirement that these institutions organise internal quality assurance procedures and be subject to external quality audit is a restriction on traditional academic freedom. The 1997 Universities Act acknowledged the university's "right and responsibility to preserve and promote the traditional principles of academic freedom in the conduct of its internal and external affairs". Indeed it stated that:

> a member of the academic staff of a university shall have the freedom, within the law, in his or her teaching, research and any other activities either in or outside the university, to question and test received wisdom, to put forward new ideas and to state controversial or unpopular opinions and shall not be disadvantaged, or subject to less favourable treatment by the university, for the exercise of that freedom.

However, the Act also placed certain explicit restrictions on the university's regulation of its affairs by requiring it to do so having regard to:

1. "the promotion and preservation of equality of opportunity and access

2. the effective and efficient use of resources, and

3. its obligations as to public accountability".

Furthermore, under the terms of the same Act, the university was required to prepare a strategic development plan, report on its progress after three years, "establish procedures for quality assurance aimed at improving the quality of education and related services provided by the university" and prepare policies in relation to:

1. "access to the university and to university education by economically or socially disadvantaged people, by people who have a disability and by people from sections of society significantly under-represented in the student body, and

2. equality, including gender equality, in all activities of the university".

Under the Act the university was also required to keep accounts and records in a form approved by the HEA. Thus the Act set boundary conditions, even limitations, on the university's academic freedom.

The Qualifications (Education and Training) Act 1999 similarly set the conditions and limitations of the academic freedom of the institutes of technology.

GOVERNANCE OF HIGHER EDUCATION

Given the new and changing societal context, higher education governance and management structures must adapt in order to cope with and meet the challenges. In this regard clear lines of responsibility and reporting mechanisms, well documented procedures for all participants, transparency within the institution and to the society it serves and regular feedback between all participants are the features of the approach required.

In shaping and reshaping the higher education institution for its modern task, a range of new priorities are coming to the fore, together with new definitions of its purpose. The institution's commitment to its students, its programme mix, its staff and their development, and its physical improvement, is given increasing emphasis. The use of the most appropriate technology by the institution and the optimal exploitation of advanced technology can become a hallmark of its character. Its drive to enhance its external links to society — local, national and international — in order to improve the flexibility of its response to societal needs, is also a key element of its mission.

Teamwork and partnership at department, faculty and institutional levels are vital to all the activities of the higher education institution and especially to quality assurance. The principles of team formation, management and development must underpin the approach to encouraging the human resources of the institution. Such an approach allows complementary talents to contribute more than the sum of the individual talents. It is based on the conscious development of shared values, shared purpose and loyalty to the institution and its mission among staff and students as well as loyalty of the institution to its students and staff. It seeks to constantly improve morale throughout the institution.

At all stages in the career of a staff member — recruitment and induction, staff evaluation and development, career planning, recognition of achievement and reward, promotion — measures must be taken to incorporate them into different teams to allow them to bloom. Usually a team starts as a group of individuals who over time develop trust, friendly relationships and mutual acceptance of strengths and weaknesses as well as the knowledge and capacity to work as a unit. Each such team is thus a learning unit within the overall learning organisation.

CONCLUSIONS

In this age of accountability, higher education in Ireland is now embarking on quality assurance and quality improvement as primary mechanisms and measures of this accountability. The government, and the society it represents, is demanding the achievement of excellence from higher education institutions, educators, students and graduates. Quality assurance is to be a key tool in the educational processes of these institutions, ensuring that they adequately fulfil these demands and needs of society and continue to justify the eminent role they play in Irish society.

Bibliography

An Roinn Oideachais, *Education for a Changing World* (Baile Átha Cliath: Oifig an tSoláthair) 1992

An Roinn Oideachais, Government White Paper, *Charting our Education Future* (Baile Átha Cliath: Oifig an tSoláthair) 1995

Australian Quality Council, *Program of Courses* (St. Leonards, NSW, Australia) 1995

AVEC, *Research and Consultancy in the VEC Colleges* (Dublin) 1982

Barnett, R, "Beyond Competence" in Coffield, F and W Williamson (eds), *Repositioning Higher Education* (Buckingham: Open University Press) 1997

Barnett, R, *Higher Education: a Critical Business* (Buckingham: Society for Research into Higher Education and Open University Press) 1997

Bauer, M, "Evaluation in Swedish Higher Education: Recent Trends and the Outlines of a Model", *European Journal of Education* (1988) No. 23

Bell, J, *Doing your Research Project* (Buckingham: Open University Press) 2nd edition, 1993

Blaxter, L, C Hughes and M Tight, *How to Research* (Buckingham: Open University Press) 1996

Bok, D, *Beyond the Ivory Tower: Social Responsibilities of the Modern University* (Cambridge, MA: Harvard University Press) 1982

Brown, G, "Effective Teaching" in Ellis, R (ed), *Quality Assurance for University Teaching* (Buckingham: Society for Research into Higher Education) 1993

Clancy, P, "The Evolution of Policy in Third-level Education" in Mulcahy, D G and D O'Sullivan (eds), *Irish Education Policy: Process and Substance* (Dublin: Institute of Public Administration) 1989

Clancy, P, *Access to College: Patterns of Continuity and Change* (Dublin: Higher Education Authority) 1995

Clancy, P, *Who goes to College? A Second National Survey of Participation in Higher Education* (Dublin: Higher Education Authority) 1988

Cobban, A B, *The Medieval English University, Oxford and Cambridge to c. 1500* (Berkeley: University of California Press) 1988

Commission on Higher Education 1960–1967, I. *Presentation and Summary of Report* (Baile Átha Cliath: Oifig an tSoláthair) 1967

Committee of University Chairmen, *Guide for Members of Governing Bod-*

ies of Universities and Colleges in England and Wales (London) 1995

Committee on Higher Education, Cmnd 2154, *Higher Education* (London: HMSO) 1963

Coolahan, J, *Irish Education: History and Structure* (Dublin: Institute of Public Administration) 1981

Council of Europe, *European Convention on the Academic Recognition of University Qualifications* (Strasbourg) 1971

Creme, P and M R Lea, *Writing at University: a Guide for Students* (Buckingham: Open University Press) 1997

Crosby, P, *Quality without Tears* (New York: McGraw Hill) 1984

Cryer, P, *Guidelines on the Quality Assurance of Research Degrees* (London: Higher Education Quality Council) 1996

Cryer, P, *The Research Student's Guide to Success* (Buckingham: Open University Press) 1996

Dearing, R, *Higher Education in the Learning Society,* Report of the National Committee of Inquiry into Higher Education (London) 1997

Delamont, S, P Atkinson and O Parry, *Supervising the PhD* (Buckingham: Open University Press) 1997

Deming, W E, *Quality, Productivity and Competitive Position* (Cambridge, MA: MIT Press) 1982

Dublin Institute of Technology, *Course Quality Assurance Handbook* (Dublin) 2nd edition, 1997

Dublin Institute of Technology, *General Assessment Regulations* (Dublin) 1st edition, 1998

Dublin Institute of Technology, *Regulations for Postgraduate Study by Research* (Dublin) 2nd edition, 1997

Ellis, R, "Quality Assurance for University Teaching: Issues and Approaches" in Ellis, R (ed), *Quality Assurance for University Teaching* (Buckingham: Society for Research into Higher Education) 1993

Entwistle, N and H Tait, "Approaches to Learning, Evaluation of Teaching and Preferences for Contrasting Academic Environments", *Higher Education* (1990) No. 19

Entwistle, N, *Styles of Learning* (Chichester: John Wiley and Sons) 2nd edition, 1988

European Association of Institutions of Higher Education (Eurashe), *Quality Management and Quality Assurance in European Higher Education, Methods and Mechanisms*, 1993

European Centre for the Development of Vocational Training (CEDEFOP), "Higher Education Systems in the European Union Member States: Background Note", *Vocational Training European Journal* (1997) No. 10

European Commission, *European Credit Transfer System, Users' Guide* (Brussels) 1995

European Commission, *Socrates: European Pilot Project for Evaluating Quality in Higher Education*, European Report (Brussels) 1995

European Commission, *Socrates: Initiatives of Quality Assurance and Assessment of Higher Education in Europe* (Brussels) 1995

HBO Expert Group, *Method for the Improvement of the Quality of Higher Education in Accordance with the EFQM Model* (Gröningen) 1998

Higher Education Authority, *A Comparative International Assessment of the Organisation, Management and Funding of University Research in Ireland and Europe,* Report of the CIRCA Group Europe (Dublin) 1996

Higher Education Authority, *A National Council for Educational Awards and a College of Higher Education at Limerick* (Dublin) 1969

Higher Education Authority, *Report of the Steering Committee on the Future Development of Higher Education (Based on a Study of Needs to the Year 2015)* (Dublin) 1995

Higher Education Funding Councils, *Research Assessment Exercise* (London) 1994

Higher Education Quality Council, *Guidelines on Quality Assurance* (London) 1996

Higher Education Quality Council, *Guidelines on the Quality Assurance of Research Degrees* (London) 1996

Higher Education Quality Council, *Learning from Audit 2* (London) 1996

Higher Education Quality Council, *Notes for the Guidance of Auditors* (London) 1995

Industrial Policy Review Group, *A Time for Change: Industrial Policy for the 1990s* (Baile Átha Cliath: Oifig an tSoláthair) 1992

International Organisation for Standardisation: ISO 8402, *Quality Management and Quality Assurance — Vocabulary* (Geneva) 1994

Jarratt, S A, *Report of the Steering Committee for Efficiency Studies in Universities,* Committee of Vice-Chancellors and Principals (CVCP) of the Universities of the United Kingdom (London) 1985

Kouzes, J M and B Z Posner, *The Leadership Challenge* (San Francisco: Jossey-Bass Publishers) 2nd edition, 1995

Levy, J, "Engineering Education in the United Kingdom: Standards, Quality Assurance and Accreditation", *International Journal of Engineering Education* (2000) 16(2)

Liaison Committee of Rectors' Conferences, *Quality Assessment in European Higher Education* (Brussels) 1992

Magennis, S, "Appraisal Schemes and their Contribution to Quality in Teaching" in Ellis, R (ed), *Quality Assurance for University Teaching* (Buckingham: Society for Research into Higher Education) 1993

McDonagh, P, *Emerging Issues in Quality Assurance in Irish Higher Education,* Seminar on Self-Regulatory Approach to Quality Assurance in Dublin Institute of Technology (Dublin) May 1994

McGrath, F, *Newman's University: Ideas and Reality* (Dublin) 1951

Melody, W, "Universities and Public Policy" in Smith, A and F Webster (eds), *The Postmodern University? Contested Visions of Higher Education in*

Society (Buckingham: Society for Research into Higher Education and Open University Press) 1997

Moed, H F and A M Ramaekers, *Bibliometric Profiles of Academic Biology Research in the Netherlands*, Report to the Association of Universities in the Netherlands (VSNU) (Leiden: Netherlands Quality Assessment of Research) 1994

Moed, H F and J G van der Velde, *Bibliometric Profiles of Academic Chemistry Research in the Netherlands*, Report to Netherlands Foundation for Chemical Research, Centre for Science and Technology, 1993

Mulcahy, D G and D O'Sullivan (eds), *Irish Educational Policy: Process and Substance* (Dublin: Institute of Public Administration) 1989

National Agency for Higher Education, *The Current System of Quality Assurance in Sweden* (Stockholm) 1995

National Council for Educational Awards, *Examinations Marks and Standards 1998* (Dublin) 1998

National Education Convention Secretariat, *Report on the National Education Convention* (Dublin) 1994

O'Sullivan, B, *Personal Communication* (Dublin: Dublin Institute of Technology) 1999

Oakland, J S, *Total Quality Management* (Oxford: Heinemann Professional) 1989

OECD, *Education at a Glance* (Paris) 1995

OECD, *Universities under Scrutiny* (Paris) 1987

Phillips, E M, and D S Pugh, *How to get a PhD: a Handbook for Students and Supervisors* (Buckingham: Open University Press) 2nd edition, 1994

Phillips, W M, G D Peterson and K B Aberle, "Quality Assurance for Engineering Education in a Changing World", *International Journal of Engineering Education* (2000) 16(2)

Skilbeck, M and H Connell, "Industry-University Partnerships in the Curriculum: Trends and Developments in the OECD Countries", *Industry and Higher Education* (Feb 1996)

Smith, A and F Webster (eds), *The Postmodern University? Contested Visions of Higher Education in Society* (Buckingham: Society for Research into Higher Education and Open University Press) 1997

Sterian, P E, *Accreditation and Quality Assurance in Higher Education*, Papers on Higher Education, CEPES (UNESCO) 1992

Stokes, P A and M McGarry, *Supply and Demand for IT Personnel in Ireland 1996-2000* (Dublin) 1996

Teastas, *First Report* (Dublin) 1997

Technological Education, Report of the International Study Group to the Minister for Education, 1987

Thackwray, B and H Hamblin, "Total Quality Management, Investors in People and Higher Education", *Engineering Science and Education Journal* (June 1996)

Throw, M, *Managerialism and the Academic Profession: The Case of England, The Quality Debate*, Times Education Supplement Seminar (Milton Keynes) 1993

van Vught, F A and D F Westerheijden, *Quality Management and Quality Assurance in European Higher Education: Methods and Mechanisms*, Center for Higher Education Policy Studies, University of Twente, 1993

van Vught, F A, "Intrinsic and Extrinsic Aspects of Quality Assessment in Higher Education" in Westerheijden, D F et al. (eds), *Changing Contexts of Quality Assessment* (Utrecht: LEMMA) 1994

Vroeijenstijn, A I, *Current Dutch Policy Towards Assessing Quality in Higher Education*, 5th International Conference on Assessing Quality in Higher Education (Bonn) 1993

Vroeijenstijn, A I, *Methodology and Implementation of Quality Assurance in Higher Education — the Netherlands Experience*, Seminar on Self-Regulatory Approach to Quality Assurance in Dublin Institute of Technology (Dublin) 1994

Winterhager, M, "Towards Bibliometric Object: a Relational View to ISI's Science Citation Index" in van Raan, A F et al., *Science and Technology in a Policy Context* (Leiden: DSWO Press) 1991

Index